THE TRANSFORMING PATH

Also by Terry Wardle:

Draw Close to the Fire: Finding God in the Darkness

Whispers of Love in Seasons of Fear

Wounded: How to Find Wholeness and Inner Healing through Him

The Soul's Journey into God's Embrace

Healing Care, Healing Prayer: Helping the Broken Find Wholeness in Christ

THE TRANSFORMING PATH

*A Christ-Centered Approach
to Spiritual Formation*

Terry Wardle

LEAFWOOD
PUBLISHERS

THE TRANSFORMING PATH
published by Leafwood Publishers

Copyright © 2003 by Terry Wardle

ISBN 0-9728425-0-0
Printed in the United States of America

Cover design by Rick Gibson

For information:
Leafwood Publishers, Siloam Springs, Arkansas
1-877-634-6004 (toll free)
www.leafwoodpublishers.com

05 06 07 08   9 8 7 6 5 4 3 2

To Aaron and Destry
and your precious gift of Grace

Contents

1 / The Christian Journey

In recent years I regularly find myself off alone, deep in thought about my past. It may involve a long, slow walk through our town, or an afternoon sitting in a quite place where no one can disturb me. When the weather is cooperative, I often lie in my hammock looking into the sky, reflecting upon all that has been. I am sure that growing older motivates some of this. In part I do it because it might help me better anticipate the future. But mostly I simply look back to remember the people and events that God has used to shape me during my twenty-five years of faith. And whenever I do, a wide range of emotions surface from a place deep within my soul.

On the one hand, I come alive with feelings of gratitude and joy. I look to the past and am reminded that the Lord has been immeasurably good to me. I have received countless mercies from His hand, and blessings more than I am able to number. He has used both successes and failures to change me, and in spite of my weakness He has been gracious, abundantly gracious. I have been allowed to serve the Lord in ways I had never dreamed possible, with some of the most wonderful people in the world. And there has been good fruit. It is impossible for me to think about these things without welling up with great emotion. The experience is humbling and exciting at the same time. Sometimes there are even tears.

On the other hand, reflecting on my past unleashes sadness, frustration, and even anger. I recognize that there are several reasons for these feelings. Some of the emotion is rooted in deep wounds that occurred during dark and difficult seasons in my Christian life. The Lord continues to heal these memories and redeem them for good. I have written about this part of my journey in previous books.[1] I know that part of the sadness comes from recalling my own failures and poor choices. The Lord never fails to remind me that His grace has been and always will be sufficient for such wanderings. But a considerable amount of the emotional reaction I experience stems back to my initiation into the Christian life over a quarter of a century ago. In retrospect I see that the Christian life has not been exactly what people told me it would be.

The "evangelists" who explained the way of Christ to me clearly and accurately set forth the call to repentance and belief, for which I will be eternally grateful. But their description of being a Christian spoke almost exclusively of joy, victories, power to do "all things" and a life of mountain-top faith, all portrayed as normative for the faithful believer. Frankly, that has not been my experience. Certainly there have been such times, but there has also been great trial, difficulty, and even doubt. By their description the only conclusion to be drawn from my facing such events was that there must have been something wrong with me.

For many years I saw such struggles as indictments of my own weakness and frailty. This would often begin a dark cycle of self-contempt, followed by more striving and effort, which produced little measurable result, for which I would again beat myself for being such a failure. Granted, I do not always get it right. However, I have come to see that the presence of tough times is not always a result of a Christian's inability to walk perfectly before the Lord. Time, scripture, and the testimony of many who have gone before have taught me that the Christian life includes more than mountain-top experiences. There are valleys, as well as deserts and dark places along the way. That is simply a fact of the life of faith and should be clearly explained to every follower of Christ. Such times and places come regardless of a person's level of sinfulness or sainthood. The teaching that a new believer receives should include clear instruction regarding the place of difficulty, doubt, and trial in forming a person in Christ Jesus.

A new believer should receive clear instruction regarding the place of difficulty, doubt, and trial in forming a person in Christ Jesus.

Upon accepting Christ I was discipled in a conservative evangelical congregation. I received many blessings from this family of believers that have served me well throughout the years. They were dedicated men and women who believed that they were preparing new believers for the Christian life. But in retrospect, the priorities that they emphasized did not prepare me adequately for the journey I faced as a Christian. What they taught me was important, but inadequately and insufficiently developed relative to darkness and difficulty.

I was told that knowing what I believed was more important than anything else for living a successful Christian life. So I set about learning great amounts of theology, apologetics, and Christian doctrine. Again, this is not unimportant knowledge. Unfortunately the approach was far more oriented to the classroom than life. I got the impression that I was headed for some final exam where knowing all this information would be required to graduate to a higher level. It seemed that if I did not know the right answer I would surely fail the test of faith. As a result, while I had a great amount of knowledge related to the Christian life, I was unable to integrate it into the actual issues I faced as a sojourner through often difficult terrain.

While my notebook was full of sound doctrine, my life presented questions that were left unaddressed. This was particularly true when the landscape grew dark and raised deep questions of doubt. It seemed that even talking about such things was wrong. As a result I faltered along the path when I faced these feelings. I did not know that countless men and women before me had walked that same, troubling way. The insights of these fellow pilgrims were not shared with me and as a result I was left to wander, unaware that they had written of these things.

Behavior modification was another key part of my early training. Soon after becoming a Christian I was presented with a list of do's and don'ts for proper Christian living. The implication was clear; good Christians live according to these standards and modify their behaviors accordingly. I could see that some of these requirements were clearly reflected in scripture, while others did not seem nearly as obvious. Regardless, I quickly caught on that belonging to that group of believers depended upon my ability to walk the line. I saw the reactions that came when someone "backslid," and I did not want to experience the rejection it brought. So, with all that I had within I tried to behave properly, finding it necessary at times to hide my struggles until I overcame the "trial." That seldom worked. It did not take long for me to realize that the ability to change my behavior was not an indication of genuine character transformation. This was especially obvious when life was tough, for it was much harder to pretend to be something I was not when the heat became unbearable.

Finally, I was taught that service was a critical part of the Christian experience. I still believe that, but sense frustration when I reflect on the way ministry was first presented to me as part of the Christian life. Involvement in Christian ministry was performance driven. I was to serve because it identified me as a sold out, first class, grade A follower of Christ. I was taught that it was better to burn out for the Lord than rust out, so from the outset I was determined to give my all. I wanted to be somebody and fell into the trap of trying to gain that acceptance through serving the Lord and accomplishing great things for the kingdom. I did accomplish a lot and more than a few applauded my efforts, advancing me into even greater responsibilities. But my drive to succeed was a grand prelude to failure, for I had become barren deep within while trying to bear great fruit for God and His kingdom.

I do not want someone to think that I do not appreciate the importance of correct Christian beliefs, proper Christian behavior, and effective Christian service. Each of these is a vital part of the life of faith, if and when they are taught from the proper perspective. But the approach must go far beyond preparing a person for some final exam that evaluates right standing with God, or a trial where people are judged according to a standard of proper behavior, or a performance review necessary for some type of ecclesiastical promotion. I can testify that this only leads to a performance based, shallow substitute for Christianity that lacks genuine power and relevance. It does not anticipate the true nature of the Christian pilgrimage, which prioritizes intimacy with the Lord Jesus Christ along a journey through life that can be utterly transformational.

The true path of faith is far from easy, and regardless of what some say, it will invariably take the pilgrim through places of great struggle, occasional darkness, and at times suffocating doubt. But this need not take a person by surprise. From the very first day of faith the Christian can be assured that this is truly the way of Jesus. He has gone before us to prepare the way, and by looking at His life we can best anticipate the journey. He has also promised to be with us in increasing levels of intimate relationship regardless of the terrain. And, by God's grace, we will be continuously transformed into the likeness of the very One who is both the means and end of this journey of faith, Jesus Christ our Lord.

The Christian Life as a Journey

The best and most biblical metaphor for understanding the Christian life is the "journey." Consider Abraham. God called him to leave his homeland and journey with Him to a new and better place. God promised Abraham that he would become a great nation, be blessed of the Lord, and in turn be a blessing to others (Gen. 12:1-4). The pilgrimage Abraham made with God was far from easy. It took a long time to reach the land of promise and all along the way Abraham faced great challenges. Abraham made many good decisions as he moved toward Canaan, but also experienced failure and setback. Sometimes he walked patiently, waiting for God to fulfill His promises. At other times, as with the birth of Ishmael, he took things into his own hands and ended up with more trouble than he could have imagined. There were places along the journey where Abraham experienced rest and abundance. At others locations on the path he would cry out for divine intervention as his very life seemed threatened. Through it all, God was shaping Abraham, transforming him into the father of a great nation. The journey was an instrument of change in Abraham's life, God's way of making him the celebrated man of faith written of in Hebrews 11.

Moses and the children of Israel were a pilgrim people.

After 400 years of cruel bondage, God called Moses to lead the chosen people back to the land of promise. Moses was prepared for this role by his own private journey into the desert, where God formed him into the deliverer. When the time was right God met Moses at the burning bush and called him to lead the Israelites to the land of milk and honey. With that call Moses began a new journey that would last 40 years and involve many trials and tribulations along the way. Each step was led by God and used to prepare the Israelites to be His people. When the Israelites chose obedience, they saw the miraculous hand of God at work on their behalf and they walked in victory. When they responded to the challenges of the journey with angry rebellion, they faced the heartache and loss of devastating defeat. Through it all, God was shaping a people for himself. Every step along the way held the potential to be an instrument of transformation, each trial an opportunity for growth, and every enemy threat an occasion to become stronger in the Lord. Nothing was lost to the redeeming purposes of God as long as the people responded with willing and surrendered hearts. The path led to more than the land of promise. It led the Israelites to the glorious inheritance of God's chosen people.

Like Abraham, Moses, the children of Israel, and a host of others throughout history, Christians today are to be a pilgrim people. We are invited to journey through life with Jesus Christ and be continuously changed by the power of His presence. That is the incredible reality of the life of faith. Being a Christian is immeasurably more than right belief, acceptable behavior, and effective service. Being a Christian is saying yes to daily fellowship and empowerment with the Lord. We are not headed for some great test or evaluation in heaven. We are destined for the bridal chamber, and every day presents an opportunity to encounter the One who loves us like no other.

Christ promises believers that He will accompany them on the journey. He told his followers two thousand years ago that he would be with them always, and that commitment stands. He did not say that the pilgrimage would be an easy one. To the contrary. He said that this world would bring trouble to His disciples. There will be trials and difficulties. The journey will take people across deserts and darkness. The winds of doubt will blow and there will be battles. But the encouragement He offers is this: "be of good cheer, for I have overcome the world" (John 16:33).

> *The wise believer has one great desire—to become "Christ possessed."*

The glory of the Christian life is not found in the promise of victories or a life of ease or a perpetual state of mountain-top ecstasy. The gift of faith is Christ himself. It is Jesus, who is within, before, and behind, walking through life as our constant companion and strength. The wise believer recognizes that the treasure is Christ, and he or she has one great desire—to become "Christ possessed."

Recently a student took exception to this notion, saying that too much emphasis was placed upon the relational nature of Christian experience. I could not disagree more. The invitation to be in relationship with Christ on the journey through life is what Christianity is all about. Jesus died so that we who were once far away from God could be brought near. Jesus did not die on a cross to give me a Bible and sound theology. He shed His blood so that I could be united with God and transformed by the power of His love, which is Jesus Christ.

Growing Along the Path

I believe that "journey" Christians will experience growth in four areas as they commit to following Christ along life's path. First and foremost, believers have the opportunity to experience increasing levels of intimacy with the Lord. As Christians move along the path with Christ, they are drawn into deeper experiences of love and intimate embrace with their Eternal Lover. How does that happen? Every time Christians turn to Christ for guidance and strength, their relationship with Jesus grows. When trials come, difficulties threaten to overrun, and doubts assail, wise pilgrims look to the Lord. Soon they find that they receive more than help in such moments. They become more deeply bonded to Christ. In time, the glory of the journey is not simply the help He brings, but the satisfying experience of His presence. Jesus told His followers that knowing him was the key to eternal life, and the relationship he was referring to was full of love and tenderness (John 17:3). We were made for such intimacy and are never satisfied with substitutes, regardless of how important they seem to be. We want Christ.

There is a second area of growth for those who walk through life with the Lord, and that is conformity to Christ. The Apostle Paul wrote in his letter to the Romans that God has a grand purpose for every believer. He said that "those God foreknew He predestined to be conformed to the likeness of His Son" (Rom. 8:28). God's plan of redemption includes transforming sinful, broken people into men and women who reflect the very nature of Christ in their lives. And amazingly, this is something He is committed to accomplishing in believers lives by His power, not theirs. Paul wrote that Christians will be conformed, not strive to conform themselves. In his letter to the Philippians Paul wrote, "he who began a good work in you will carry it on to completion until the day of Christ Jesus" (Phil. 1:6). How does

God do this? He uses every moment of every day, each trial the believer faces, and any and all opportunities that come along the path of life.

Third, walking through life with Jesus also provides Christians with opportunities to recognize their identity in Christ. Innumerable believers struggle with feelings of unworthiness, insecurity, and abandonment. Often they try to gain some sense of personal worth and acceptance through performance or people pleasing. But in the end they become painfully aware that such behaviors offer only temporary relief and long-term feelings of despair and depression. But the battle for meaning and worth has already been won for every believer by Jesus Christ. Christians are "new creations in Christ Jesus" (II Cor. 5:17), and have been given an identity as "children of God." The scriptures refer to believers as salt, light, saints, citizens of heaven, overcomers, God's workmanship, and the bride of Christ. This new identity is true of all Christians, beginning the very moment they choose to follow Christ. And the landscape of the journey is used by God to help them discover who they truly are, in spite of trial and turmoil, and walk as precious sons and daughters of God.

Finally, following Jesus on the journey of life provides Christians with daily opportunities to grow and develop as disciples. They will experience increasing levels of intimacy, ongoing conformity, and deepening confidence in their new Christian identity. There will also be opportunities to mature as wounded healers of Christ. The wounds of Christ are precious to all who believe, for from those wounds flow the healing grace that we all so desperately need. Jesus gave His body and shed His blood so that broken people everywhere could experience new life. And on the journey with Christ, believers learn that Jesus calls them to the same ministry. Every struggle and challenge they face prepares them for this divinely appointed ministry. As Christians encounter pain and trial with Christ's help, they grow in their ability to serve others who will walk that same difficult path. Where believers have received comfort in struggle, they are able to turn and offer that experience as an instrument of help and healing. Christians who have been wounded experience the power of Christ flowing through their hurts to touch countless other people in need.

People who follow Jesus in life will be changed. They will grow because God has committed to using all that life brings as an opportunity for His transforming touch. This process of development does not happen as a result of striving or effort, but as an act of His incredible grace upon the people He loves. Certainly there are things believers need to know in order to cooperate with God along the path. Understanding and submitting to these truths will position them for all that God wants to do.

What Does the Pilgrim Need to Know?

There are certain things that Christians should know about walking the path of faith with Jesus. First, the journey is not a quick trip. There may be instant cash, instant credit, and instant food. But there is no instant intimacy with Christ, or conformity to His image, or security in His identity, or maturity as His wounded healer. This level of spiritual maturity happens over time. The Christian experience is a lifelong pilgrimage where believers follow step by step behind the Lord. Anyone who thinks that the path of faith is a quick sprint down a hundred meter track will burn out long before reaching the finish line. It is a journey that includes every second, minute, hour, day, month, and year of the believer's life.

Second, the Christian who walks with Jesus through life must know that change is a process. When I was a young believer I attended a camp meeting where the speaker invited all who wanted to be sanctified to walk forward for special prayer. I was thrilled to think that somehow God was

going to supernaturally move me to a life of newfound holi-
ness and obedience. I did experience Jesus at that altar rail
those many years ago, but I have found that my struggles did
not disappear. Change happens over time, involving many
different truths, experiences, and people along the way. It is
not unlike baking something that takes the interaction of
many different ingredients to bring about the desired end.
Christians will find that while some change happens easily,
most comes slowly, through a process of development that
bears fruit in due season.

Third, God uses everything that happens to the Christian
along the journey of faith as an instrument of development
and change. The promise of Romans 8:29 teaches believers
that God has chosen Christians to be conformed to the image
of Christ. What does He use in that process? The previous
verse holds the answer. "We know that in all things God works
for the good of those who love Him" (Rom. 8:28). Believers
who follow after Christ must come to recognize the power of
this "all things" principle. Christians are transformed by God as
they move forward in life and everything that happens to them
is part of that process. Everything. Not just the good times,
moments of obedience, and obvious successes along the way.
God is also present in the tough times, the sinful choices, and
the failures that are an inevitable part of the journey. This is a
vital principle of Christian development. God's grace is grand
enough to redeem every moment in life for the purpose of
Christian growth. Faithful pilgrims must learn to find the Lord
in the present moment and allow Him to use it for His eternal
purpose.

Fourth, followers of Christ must daily surrender the events
of life to the transforming touch of God. Years ago I was
trapped in a season of debilitating depression. All of life
seemed to lose meaning and I found the simplest activities of
life too much to bear. I had to be hospitalized for almost a

month, which was in itself a very painful trial. I remember sitting on my bed the first night engulfed in fear and weeping. Suddenly these words from Corrie Ten Boon ran across my mind: "The object of your greatest pain can become the source of your greatest blessing if you give it to God." Somehow those words went deep and I surrendered the nightmare I was trapped in for the Lord's purposes. Those years were far from easy and more than once I wanted to give up. But the Lord met me in the struggle and brought a personal transformation that is beyond words. Today I give constant testimony that Corrie's words are a reality. If Christians hold any hope of walking through life victoriously, they must learn the constant discipline of surrender.

Fifth, the journey with Jesus is empowered by the presence of His Holy Spirit within the believer's life. I learned the

---

God uses everything that happens to the Christian as an instrument of development and change.

---

hard way that the Christian life cannot be lived in a person's own strength. Any effort to do so inevitably ends in frustration and failure. Trying to follow Jesus without the Spirit's indwelling empowerment is like trying to cross the ocean in a sailboat by blowing on the sails. It is impossible, and more importantly, because of Christ's provision, totally unnecessary. Jesus has given His Holy Spirit to help every believer and that Spirit will provide the power to move forward along the path. Knowing this in theory is not enough for the pilgrim. He or she must grow to experientially recognize the presence of the Holy Spirit, and obediently rely upon His guidance and empowerment every day. The believer's path will often cross terrain that seems impossible to traverse. Only the Person of the Holy Spirit can empower people to move forward with Jesus into tomorrow.

Finally, followers of Christ will constantly face choices along the path. Almost every day believers will come to some fork in the road and be confronted with a choice. They will be challenged either to take the path Christ walked, which is seldom easy, or follow the way of least resistance. The crowd will pressure Christians, trying to lure them away from the upward path. All the while Jesus will quietly summon them to trust Him and follow along the less traveled way. These choices are critical to spiritual development, for they position pilgrims either to become more like Jesus or more like the world.

The decisions do not change people, but rather position them to be changed by the power of the one they follow. If Christians choose the path of Christ, His presence will transform them. If they choose to go an easier way, the power of the world will bring its own change to bear. In time, regardless of the chosen path, another fork in the road will appear that holds the same opportunity for formation. And once again pilgrims must choose Jesus. If a wrong path has been taken, at the next fork believers need to choose Him again, for Jesus will yet again stand before all pilgrims and beckon them to walk His way.

So What Do I Need To Do?

When I share these concepts I receive questions about what a Christian needs to do to successfully make this journey. That is an important question, though a secondary one. I always encourage disciples to get into God's word regularly, spend time with other believers, learn the basic beliefs of the faith and practice spiritual disciplines as the Lord leads. All of this is valuable and proves helpful as long as the paradigm of learning is "journey" sensitive and not a modernistic exercise in intellectual gymnastics. Spiritual formation and Christian practice must be presented in a way that helps people follow Christ and grow in relationship to Him.

I believe that there is a far more important question for "journey" Christians to ask—and this question serves as the focus of the remainder of this book: "What should Christians expect to face along the path of life when they choose to follow Christ?" Granted, the Christian journey is not easily mapped nor is it predictable enough to provide a generic "trip-tik" that can adequately serve everyone. But given the reality of so much challenge, trial, and battle, is there not some way to anticipate what lies ahead? I am convinced that there is a place to look that will serve as a wonderful guide to all serious pilgrims. Since Jesus is the One we Christians are to follow along the path of life, shouldn't His own journey serve to prepare and instruct believers for their life-long pilgrimage? The answer is yes. Jesus who leads the way for us has walked this journey successfully and, by looking at what He faced along the way, we can gain valuable insights into the landscape and challenge of our own journeys.

Knowing my own need for guidance on the Christian journey, the Holy Spirit, I believe, led me into the gospels of Christ to show me a series of pathways that Christians will inevitably face as they move through life with Christ. Jesus walked through them all and now seeks to invite believers to take these paths on their own journey of transformation. By considering these pathways, Christians can better recognize what lies before them and prepare to choose Christ's way rather than the way of least resistance. I have alliterated these pathways and identify each with a simple word:

Conception
Community
Confrontation
Consecration
Construction
Commission
Credentialing
Conflict
Communicating
Communion
Compassion
Confusion
Cross
Crown

Each pathway is taken from the life of Christ and will be discussed in the following chapters. I am proposing a process of spiritual development centered upon the life and person of Jesus Christ. We will look to Christ in order to anticipate following Christ on a journey that unites us more deeply with Him and transforms us more and more into His image.

Before moving ahead there are two final considerations. First, these pathways will not necessarily be encountered in the order presented. The Holy Spirit will guide each person along the way best suited. However, I do believe that somewhere along the journey, every Christian will encounter each of the choices outlined here. Second, I have found that people come to choices and challenges similar to those they faced in the past. Why? Because there is a deeper work yet to be done. Obedient surrender will always be a necessary stance for the faithful pilgrim.

In this very moment Jesus stands before us lovingly extending His hand and beckoning us to follow. If we listen to our heart, we will go with Him, for deep within we know that

Jesus is the Treasure we have longed to embrace. Jesus, the Eternal Lover, invites us to join Him on a transformational journey that will move forward gloriously into all eternity. He whispers, "Come, follow me." And with that invitation, we begin.

Note

1. This part of my own story is contained in *Wounded: How to Find Healing and Inner Wholeness Through Him* and *Draw Close to the Fire: Finding God in the Darkness.*

2 / Conception

G od is breathtakingly self-giving, and nowhere is this more evident than in the sending of Jesus Christ. The Apostle John wrote the following words in his first epistle to the church: "God is love. This is how God showed His love among us: He sent the one and only Son into the world that we might live through Him. This is love: not that we loved God, but that He loved us and sent His Son as an atoning sacrifice for our sins" (I John 4:8-10).

People who take the time to seriously consider these words will find themselves caught up in the most wondrous story the universe has ever known. No novel, narrative, poem, or work of art captures the heartbeat of passionate love like the romance told in the pages of sacred scripture. God, longing for His lost and captive children, sends His only Son to earth, where He sacrifices His very life in order to bring broken people everywhere back into the eternal embrace of the Heavenly Father.

Christ's journey to reclaim and redeem the earth begins with the magnificent, though somewhat mystifying, story of the incarnation. Jesus, the eternal Son of God, completely empties himself of heavenly glory, and enters life on earth as a human being. He could have arrived in supernatural splendor and with a great display of power and might. But Jesus chose to come humbly. Instead of overwhelming people with resounding trumpets, blinding flashes of light, and an entourage of the heavenly host, Jesus comes in poverty, weakness, and great vulnerability. Rather than initiating His rescue mission from the throne of the most powerful nation on earth, the Son of God silently enters the womb of a simple Israelite woman named Mary.

The Incarnation

The story of the incarnation begins over two thousand years ago in the obscure town of Nazareth (Luke 1:26-38). God sent an angel, Gabriel, to deliver a most astounding message to Mary, who was engaged to a good man named Joseph. Gabriel told Mary that she was going to give birth to a son who would be called the Son of the Most High, and that he would reign over God's house forever. Mary was overwhelmed with these words and asked the angel how this could be, since she was a virgin. Gabriel described how the Holy Spirit would come upon her and she would conceive the one called "the Son of God" (Luke 1:35). While these words seemed hard to believe, Gabriel assured Mary that "nothing is impossible with God." Mary responded, "I am the Lord's servant...May it be to me as you said" (Luke 1:37-38). And with that, the angel left. Soon after Mary was found to be with child as the angel had promised. Mary, the virgin, was carrying the Christ child, and the world would be forever changed.

Two key points related to the incarnation must not be overlooked by those who choose to journey with Christ through life. First, the Holy Spirit was an active part of Jesus' entire life, beginning with the moment of conception.

Granted, it is not easy for the human mind to comprehend how the Holy Spirit overshadowed Mary to impregnate her with Jesus. But this point is clear: life for Jesus began in the Spirit and was inseparably linked to His constant presence. From conception to the cross the Holy Spirit remained a full and active participant in all that Jesus said and did.

Second, Mary also needed to be a willing participant in Christ's conception. There is an element of mystery as to why God would choose to bring his perfect Son to earth in partnership with an imperfect human being. As wonderful as the young Mary may have been, she was still a person with lim-

---

*In order to walk with Christ
and grow close to Him,
a person must be born again.*

---

itations and weaknesses. God, who is omnipresent and omnipotent, could have bypassed human involvement, initiating a plan of salvation that did not risk human bungling. Yet God chose Mary to be the mother of Jesus. God did not force her into submission, but invited her to willingly welcome the Spirit's presence within her body. She did, and Jesus was born.

Christians will find that they too will be called to participate with the Holy Spirit as they follow Christ along the journey. Like Mary, they will be invited to welcome the Holy Spirit within their lives. When they do Jesus will come alive to them and be bonded in the deepest level of relationship possible.

Born of the Spirit
Over thirty years after His birth, Jesus had a very important conversation with a religious leader named Nicodemus

(John 3:1-21). Nicodemus had seen the miracle-working power of Christ and was convinced that Jesus was sent of God. That was a very unpopular position for a member of the Pharisees to take since they openly opposed Christ. And so He came to Jesus by night in order that he would not be seen by members of his religious sect. Nicodemus said to Jesus, "Rabbi, we know that you are a teacher sent from God. For no one could perform the miraculous signs you are doing if God were not with him" (John 3:2). Jesus said, "I tell you the truth, no one can see the kingdom of God unless he is born again" (John 3:3).

Nicodemus was puzzled by Jesus' remark. Was He talking about a person reentering his mother's womb? Jesus said, "I tell you the truth, no one can enter the kingdom of God unless he is born of water and the Spirit. Flesh gives birth to flesh, but Spirit gives birth to spirit" (John 3:5, 6). Jesus was telling Nicodemus, and every person since that night, that being a member of God's family involves a spiritual birth. A true Christian is a man or woman, boy or girl, who has welcomed the Holy Spirit's indwelling presence into his or her life. Just as the Spirit conceived Jesus within Mary, so the Holy Spirit seeks to impregnate people afresh with His Presence. Those who experience this new birth find that they begin an ever-deepening relationship with the One who loves them as no other.

The spiritual experience that Jesus discussed that night with Nicodemus had been prophesied centuries earlier. God, speaking through the prophet Ezekiel, pointed to a future time when He would place a new heart and new spirit within His chosen people (Ezek. 36:26, 27). God said that He would put His Spirit in people to help them walk obediently with Him through life. I am convinced that the words the Lord spoke through Ezekiel were directly related to what Jesus told Nicodemus. Being a child of God involves a spiritual birth within a person. That experience initiates a redeemed relationship with the Father of love. And so, in order to walk with Christ and grow close to Him, a person must be born again.

Jesus repeatedly referred to the ministry of the Holy Spirit in His ministry and said that experiencing His presence was foundational to faith. He told the woman at the well that the only way to worship God was through the Spirit because God Himself is Spirit (John 4: 24). On another occasion He said, "The Spirit gives life: the flesh counts for nothing" (John 6:63). Once, when Pharisees were criticizing His ministry, Jesus said that whoever believed in Him would have streams of living water flowing from within him (John 7:38). The commentary that comes immediately after this statement made it clear that Jesus was referring to the presence of the Holy Spirit within all who follow Him (John 7:39).

Christians personally receive the Holy Spirit when they declare allegiance to Jesus Christ. This indwelling, or new birth, seals them as God's very own children and establishes a relational bond between the Christian and the Lord. Being God's adopted child brings innumerable benefits, but the relational experience is at the center of all that God gives. This relationship is the heartbeat of Christian experience and the reason for Christ dying upon a cross. Jesus did not give His life so that people could receive a new list of rules or more religious rituals. He went to Calvary so that people could be forgiven of sin and grow to experience intimate fellowship with the Father. And, according to scripture, the only way to become a child of God is through faith in Christ.

Some people try to find God by walking a different path than the one Jesus took. They think that good works or faithfully participating in religious rituals will bring them into the family of God. Some work to gain great amounts of knowledge about God, as though understanding alone could initiate a relationship with Him. Many people, even those who regularly attend a local church, try to become right with God by religiously obeying certain rules and regulations that have invariably been set up by people, not God.

Countless well meaning people seem to be trying to earn right standing with God by working tirelessly for Him. Jesus spoke clearly to this when He delivered the Sermon on the Mount. He said, "Not everyone who says to me, 'Lord, Lord,' will enter the kingdom of heaven, but only he who does the will of my Father who is in heaven. Many will say to me on that day, 'Lord, Lord, did we not prophecy in your name, and in your name drive out demons and perform many miracles?' Then I will tell them plainly, 'I never knew you. Away from

---

Works, knowledge, rules, and rituals will never re-establish lost people with the Heavenly Father.

---

me you evil doers!' (Matt. 7:21-23). When Jesus said, "I never knew you," He was talking about experiential knowledge. He was referring to the kind of "knowing" that comes through an intimate relationship between two people. Service alone does not bring that kind of "knowledge."

Jesus made it abundantly clear that the only way to have an intimate relationship with God was through a spiritual re-birth. All other efforts end in emptiness and frustration. Works, knowledge, rules, rituals will never re-establish lost people with the Heavenly Father. Anyone who follows that path will find that it dead-ends at despair, depression, and ultimate death. The Spirit alone brings life, and that life begins when a person receives Christ and commits to following after Him.

A Personal Word of Testimony

I look back at my own new birth experience with wonder and gratitude. I had repeatedly heard the gospel of Christ, but had failed to surrender to Him as Lord and Savior of my life. I wasn't interested in the claims of Christ and the path of faith. I was too busy trying to be popular, to have a good time, and to make progress along the path the world had set before me. I was caught in more than a few destructive behaviors, though at the time I believed they were bringing a certain degree of pleasure and purpose to my life. I wanted to gain friends, find a good career, earn lots of money, and enjoy the good things life had to offer. What could be wrong with that?

Over time this illusion began to collapse around me, leaving me to consider how empty my life had become. Nothing I was doing satisfied, and most of what I was about seemed ultimately meaningless. I had reached the point that many people come to in life, when there is a desperate, aching desire for something more. I, like everyone, was made to have an intimate relationship with God, and nothing apart from Him would satisfy that deep longing. And so in time I came to a fork in the road where I had an opportunity to choose. The path of least resistance was a familiar one, leading to more of what I had been experiencing in life. But there was also another way, a higher road, and on it stood Jesus inviting me to walk with Him. I knew that His way was the right choice, but felt that the demands of the journey would be too much for me. The way seemed hard and the lifestyle one that I would find difficult to live. But the word of Christ was compelling, wooing me to declare my allegiance to Him and begin a relationship that would change my life forever.

Amazingly, as I somewhat fearfully made the choice to follow Christ, an unexpected transformation took place deep inside of me. The Holy Spirit entered my life and, as Jesus had told Nicodemus, a new birth took place. God's Spirit had renewed my spirit and He set up permanent residence within. Like Mary at the incarnation, the Spirit of God brought divine life into the heart of my existence. When the invitation to receive new life was extended to me I said yes, and a new partnership began. Jesus became my Lord and Lover, and I started a journey to become His intimate beloved. I felt the presence of the Holy Spirit and just as He had promised two thousand years ago, I was born again, Spirit within spirit.

The difference was like a new dawning. Light began to break through for me and I felt alive for the very first time. I seemed to see life differently, feel differently, and hunger for things that I had never wanted before. And there was a Presence, there to teach, help, strengthen, and guide along the path. I was right when I sensed that I could not follow Jesus in my own strength. But now there was Another, there to unite me with Jesus and strengthen me for what lay ahead. The Holy Spirit had brought me to Jesus and brought Jesus to me. A new friendship was formed, a transformation begun, and a purpose for living clarified. I was made to become intimate with Christ, to become like Him, to become secure in Him, to serve as He had served. With this new birth, the journey had finally begun.

A Path to Choose

The Christian life began two thousand years ago with a divine conception in the womb of the virgin Mary. It continues today in much the same way. Jesus wants to be born in the hearts of men and women everywhere. He comes to them as Savior and Lord, the glorious Son of the Most High. Jesus does not force His way into hearts, but instead invites people to say yes. The invitation is not restricted to those who are holy and good. It is extended to the broken and lost, to the downcast and imprisoned, those who are held captive and those enslaved in cruel bondage. People who respond positively to the invitation partner with the Holy Spirit and the mystery of the incarnation happens again. A new birth takes place and a spiritual life begins to grow. It is the life of Jesus, implanted within the hearts of all who believe. This is a wonderful gift from a loving God, tenderly extended to all who want to journey in life along a new, more meaningful way.

What should people expect to face as they journey through life with Jesus Christ? As we have seen, they will repeatedly come to a fork in the road. One path will take the way of least resistance. It will be well used and deeply worn. Many will say it is the right way to travel, an easier terrain, a quicker way to go. The other path will be the way of Christ. It will not be easy and it will certainly be a more narrow way. But Jesus will be there, tenderly inviting the pilgrim to go with Him, to become His intimate friend, to grow to love more deeply, more unconditionally.

One of the very first choices the pilgrim will need to consider is this, "Will you try to find God through rules and regulations, rituals and good works? Or will you allow Jesus to be birthed anew in your life and be welcomed into an eternal relationship with Him?" This choice faces all who live the journey. And how people choose makes all the difference in life...and in death. The Holy Spirit is present, and the invitation abundantly clear: "Will you welcome the Spirit of Jesus? He longs to be born again in you."

3 / Community

How does a damp, smelly stable become one of the most celebrated places in all history? Fill it with Love.

I do not remember a time in my life when I was not aware that Jesus was born in a stable. Long before I fully understood the significance of Christmas, I knew about the manger, swaddling cloths, Mary and Joseph, shepherds, angels and three wise men from the east. As a child I remember that my family had a little nativity scene beneath our Christmas tree. There was also a large crèche displayed during the holidays in our small village. I even recall donning a bathrobe or two as a child for the seasonal Christmas pageant. The Christmas season was warm and magical to me even when I did not know what it all meant for the world.

Years later when I became a pastor I always looked forward to speaking on the Christmas message. I would preach about the young couple that made the arduous journey to Bethlehem in order to register for the Roman census, telling my people that the way to Christ is never easy, but eternally worth the trip. I talked about "no room in the inn" and challenged people to make room for the Christ-child within their own hearts. I described the angel chorus that announced the "Good News for all People," and urged listeners to join the shepherds on that journey to the manger and kneel with them in worship and adoration. Invariably there was the message about wise men, priceless gifts, and the giving of our best to the Lord. I never spoke of these things without reminding people that Jesus was born in poverty so that we could be forever enriched with eternal life. Christmas is always magical for me.

In reality, the stable was not glamorous. I have owned farm animals and know that the barn is a cold, damp, and smelly place. I appreciate the Christmas image of sheep and cattle gently lowing, but it really would have been nothing like that. Animals become noisy companions when their space is invaded and they are invariably looking for a handout. The hay would not have been soft and warm, nor would there have been a clean manger in which to place a newborn child. It would have been a tough place to give birth. And still, most any Christian would loved to have been there at the time. Why? Because when Jesus arrived two thousand years ago that stable became the center of the universe. Love itself filled the atmosphere.

I have often thought about the love that God was communicating to people that night. But until recently I did not consider the expressions of love that were directed toward the baby in the manger. This infant child had become the center of attention the moment He entered into the world. Mary and Joseph could not keep their eyes or hands off Him. The shepherds were each trying to catch a glimpse of the baby, just like relatives do today when they peer into a hospital nursery. Smiles, expressions of delight, joyful chatter, and eyes full of deep love would have been directed straight at the newborn child.

It was only a baby, and yet people were enthralled with this new life that came into the world. The baby Jesus could not do a thing by Himself, and yet He was being told that there had never been another like Him. The infant Christ needed help at every level of existence. The baby would cry at night, need regular feeding, changing, and holding. But this child was loved just because He was alive. His parents and family would have been patient, allowing Him time to grow and mature before there were any expectations of Him whatsoever. Today we can look back and say that this was all true because He deserved such love as the Son of God. But the community around Him did not see that as clearly as we do today. They were full of joy because He was a precious life with a special purpose for the world.

The experience of unconditional love begins to build a reservoir of love that is necessary for self-confidence and inner joy.

A Community of Love

Psychologists tell us that infants need to receive exactly what Jesus did in the first days and months of life: a community of relatives and friends to communicate that the child is wanted, loved, and a joy to behold. The child needs to see and feel that others experience delight when they are around. This external experience of joy begins to shape an internal reserve of joy that can be drawn from when difficult things happen in the child's life. It also helps shape ego-strength within the child, which is essential to having confidence and the initiative to attempt difficult challenges. When a child does not experience this dynamic of joy and love within the first eighteen months, the developmental process is compromised. This leads to insecurity, self-contempt, and often a latent anxiety that the child will carry through life. Instead of being able to return to the resevoir of joy built up during an "adoring infancy," the child will be stuck in fear and terror. This can lead to destructive behaviors and debilitating insecurities.

People who specialize in helping the broken are learning that those who did not receive the nurturing love they needed in infancy must enter a community of love where they can find healing. They need to get the love and touch that was withheld from them in childhood so that they can begin to love themselves. Good self-talk simply is not enough to help people who have been compromised in early development. They need to be loved, feel that they are a delight to others, and see joy in other people's eyes. The experience of unconditional love will begin to build that reservoir of love that is necessary for self-confidence and inner joy.

The same is true for the Christian journey to spiritual health and maturity. Christians, from newborns to adults, need to be part of a Christian community where love, joy, and delight are abundantly expressed. This is essential to spiritual development and to healing deep wounds that many carry in life.

Spiritual Infancy

Spiritual development requires the same community of love as psychological development. When people declare allegiance to Jesus Christ they experience the spiritual new birth that Jesus talked about with Nicodemus. And as in biological birth, they are not born spiritual adults. They are spiritual infants and demand the same joyous welcome that Jesus experienced when He came into the world. Their births should be celebrated with heavenly songs and shouts of joy.

They should be accepted into their new life with great expressions of love and excitement.

Mature Christians should go out of their way to welcome new Christians and always express delight in their membership in God's eternal family. Newborn Christians should get the impression that this community believes that the party never really begins until they are present. They should feel special, unique, and loved beyond compare. All of this will create a safe and secure place for new Christians, enabling them to grow and develop in an environment of patience and deep acceptance.

Newborn Christians also need special care. They will not get everything right and at times will require some pampering. They will not be able to feed themselves initially, and may need a lot of special attention. Their diets will be different from adults, and their stamina not nearly as hardy. But that should be fine with the community of love, because babies are special and loved just because they are alive. They will have little to offer the community at this stage, which is the way it should be with newborns. They will need to receive attention and delight from the community, and all the while get the impression that they are the most important people in the world.

Newborn Christians have a lot to learn about following Jesus, but they should never be given the impression that they are "less than" those who have walked with Christ for some time. The community that does not judge new Christians will find that new believers will be more capable of living in God's good grace. They should experience a love from the community that helps them touch the radical love that God has for each of them. They will then be increasingly secure about the fact that God is nuts about them because His community tells them that regularly.

Like any family, the community of believers will instruct newborns in the basics of Christian faith so that they will be able to follow Jesus along the journey of life. At first mature Christians will "do for" the new believer, but in a short time they will need to welcome them to participate in the matters of Christian practice, lovingly encouraging and supporting them along the way. As they grow toward increasing maturity and intimacy with the Lord, these people will take their places in the community of faith, serving with God's people as they move forward in life with Jesus Christ. This entire process builds healthy Christians who will be confident in Christ and able to return to joy when difficulty and trial assails them. This is the way of Christ, embracing new Christians into God's community of healing love.

Jesus' style of teaching and ministry was entirely relational.

Jesus and Community

The Lord Jesus was thoroughly committed to the concept of loving community. Not only did He experience that at His birth, he integrated community into His developmental years through an extended family, and into His adult life by gathering a close-knit group of followers. Soon after entering public ministry Jesus called people to be with Him as disciples. There were of course the twelve, a group of radically different men who slowly learned to love each other as they walked with Christ. But there were many others as well. The Bible also tells of women who traveled with Christ's band. And there are references to other groups, like the seventy and one hundred and twenty. All of these groups were part of Christ's new family and they learned to love as He did.

Jesus taught people kingdom principles within the context of community. They learned about the spiritual life as they walked with Him through very normal day-to-day activities. Jesus style of teaching and ministry was entirely relational. He wanted people to be "with" Him before they committed to serving Him. All they while He was delighting in them and communicating a love that would ultimately take Him to the cross in order to save them. When Jesus sent them out into ministry, He did it in groups of two and three. Being supportive of each another was important to Jesus and He wanted His followers to be unmistakably committed to that principle.

Toward the end of His earthly ministry Jesus said: "A new command I give you: Love one another. As I have loved you, love one another. By this all men will know that you are my disciples, if you love one another" (John 13:34, 35). The qualifying mark of the Christian experience is a community of Christians who love as Christ loved. All other characteristics of Christian living flow from this great commandment. If people are going to follow Christ successfully, they will do it in a community of believers who are thoroughly committed to this one law of extravagant love.

Another Crossroad

Sooner rather than later Christians will face a crossroad that will be all about Christian community. Jesus was always part of a supportive community and to follow Him will mean the same for believers. There is of course a way of least resistance. New believers could choose to isolate from others, go the way of faith alone, and never take the risk that love presents. Those who choose that path will not be betrayed by close friends, let down or disappointed by people who fail them. They will seldom experience criticism and be free to express their beliefs any way they choose. But they will also never know the wonder of being celebrated by the family of faith. They will not grow in love and live with the security and safety that comes from Christ's community. When they stumble no one will be there to help, and when they fall they will be alone in their pain. Old wounds will not receive healing and new hurts will be suffered in silent isolation. Those who make this choice will be unprotected and easy prey for forces bent on their destruction. Jesus did not go this way and it is a mistake if anyone else determines to take that path.

Jesus invites His followers to move into the community of love. He walked that path during His life on earth, and calls all Christians to go the same way. As Christians consider this choice they must recognize that not all communities calling themselves Christian express love in the manner described in this chapter. Some churches are not committed to loving newborns. They can be judgmental, critical, and impatient. Some complain that new believers do not do their part, and only show love when people perform properly. Instead of loving newborns just because they are alive, they withhold from them until they grow up. Some churches even discourage newcomers, sadly satisfied with the people they already have. Often there are lots of rules in these churches and experiences of rejection for all who fail to obey. This is very unhealthy and unquestionably not the way of Jesus.

Christians who come to the crossroad of community should be prayerful about the church or group they choose to join. While being fully committed to community, they should look for a place that shows love and acceptance to all who enter their midst. There should be a spirit of celebration in the community as well as the feeling that newborns are an absolute delight to them. The healthy Christian community will also be full of grace, patient, protective, and clearly committed to helping people grow strong in Jesus Christ. And relationship—with Jesus and with one another—must be a priority. It will not be a place where belief, behavior, and service is more important than growing closer to Christ and following Him on the journey of life. Loving Jesus will be the passion of this community and loving one another the natural outflow of that delight. And newborns are always the special people in the family.

Granted, no community will be perfect. But healthy churches are available and waiting to welcome all who choose to consider Christ as Savior and Lord of the journey. Believers must find such a place and commit to growing with other members of God's family. This choice is vitally important to spiritual life and Christian maturity. It is wonderfully inevitable that Jesus will call out, inviting the believer to join Him in community. It is a critical part of the journey. Christians should pray about this path, look for a community that reflects the love of Christ, and then give themselves wholeheartedly to Jesus and the people of faith.

4 / Consecration

To what degree, if at all, is becoming a Christian more than a private matter between God and an individual? Can't someone simply pray to receive Christ within his or her own heart, be assured of a place in heaven, and go about life as it was? These questions are important and far from rhetorical. I have been asked them many times over the years and believe the answers are foundational to what it means to be a follower of Christ.

I remember when Joe, a new believer, was headed for a weekend fishing trip with some guys at work. He had only recently come to Christ and had little knowledge of what it meant to be a Christian. He had been to church only a couple of times since experiencing the new birth, and was not sure what being a person of faith really meant. Joe and his buddies had made this trip to the Allegheny Mountains annually and generally used it as an opportunity to cut loose. In many ways their antics were harmless, but they were known to cross the line, particularly when the alcohol began to flow. When Joe decided to go with them, I determined to pray. He was a precious new brother and I wanted to lift him before the Lord for protection and strength.

When Joe returned I asked how the weekend went. He seemed to have enjoyed himself and told me about all the trout they caught along Tionesta Creek. I myself had fished that beautiful stream and felt a little envious when Joe talked about his experience. It sounded as if they had a good time. I then asked Joe how it went with his friends in light of his new faith. He seemed confused by the question.

I could tell that Joe was wondering what a fishing week-

The Christian journey calls people to move beyond private belief and to dedicate themselves publicly in the community of Christ.

---

end with friends had to do with what had happened within his own heart. He asked me what I meant by the question, so I tried to be more clear and direct. I asked Joe if anyone had inquired about his new commitment to follow Christ, or if he had found any difficulties participating in all that went on there. Suddenly he smiled and said, "Not at all. It was fine. They had no idea that I am now a Christian. I keep that between me and God."

This story cuts to the heart of a very important issue in following Christ. Is being born again simply some type of fire insurance that keeps people from going to hell? Is it a decision that is nobody's business but the one who prayed to Jesus? Or should it initiate significant change in the person's life? Should there be a more thorough-going dedication of all of life to the Lord? And if so, to what degree should that involve public declaration of faith? People have a wide range of opinions related to these questions. But I am convinced that the answer comes from God's word and is found in the life of Jesus Himself.

Dedication and Blessing

A story in scripture directly relates to the questions we are considering. It has been beautifully paraphrased in *The Message*:

> *When the eighth day arrived, the day of circumcision, the child was named Jesus, the name given by the angel before he was conceived.*
>
> *Then when the days stipulated by Moses for purification were complete, they took him up to Jerusalem to offer him to God as commanded in God's Law: "every male who opens the womb shall be an offering to God," and also to sacrifice the pair of doves or two young pigeons" prescribed in God's Law.*
>
> *In Jerusalem at the time, there was a man, Simeon by name, a good man, a man who lived in prayerful expectancy of help for Israel. And the Holy Spirit was on him. The Holy Spirit had shown him that he would see the Messiah of God before he died. Led by the Spirit, he entered the temple. As the parents of the child Jesus brought him in to carry out the rituals of the Law, Simeon took him into his arms and blessed God.*
>
> *"God, you can now release your servant: Release me in peace as you promised. With my own eyes I have seen your salvation; it is now out in the open for everyone to see: A God-revealing light to the non-Jewish nations, and of glory to your people, Israel."*
>
> *Jesus' father and mother were speechless with surprise at these words. Simeon went on to bless them and*

say to Mary his mother,

"This child marks both the failure and the recovery of many in Israel. A figure misunderstood and contradicted—- the pain of a sword-thrust through you—- But the rejection will force honesty, as God reveals who they really are."

Anna the prophetess was also there, a daughter of Phanuel form the tribe of Asher. She was now a very old woman. She had been married for seven years and a widow for eight-four. She never left the Temple area, worshipping night and day with her fastings and prayers. At the very time Simeon was praying, she showed up, broke into an anthem of praise top God, and talked about the child to all who were waiting expectantly for the freeing of Jerusalem. (Luke 2:21-38)

This story holds a great deal of truth. Some of it is related to Jesus and His relationship to the Law. While important and worth exploring, it is not the focus of my discussion. Also, many see this text as a statement about dedicating babies before the Lord after they are born. That too is an important topic, but again, not directly relevant to the point I want to address. I am sharing this story because I believe it addresses the questions I had asked Joe about his faith. It has something to say about how broad and deep a commitment to Christ should extend in the life of a believer. Four concepts stand out to me in this story, encapsulated in the words dedication, public, blessings, and praise.

When Mary and Joseph took Jesus to the temple, they were fulfilling an act of complete dedication before the Lord. God did not choose the Israelite people to be in partial relationship with Him, but complete. He was not to be God of only the religious aspects of their lives, but all of life. Their dedication to Him was not restricted to what happened in the

Temple, but impacted every moment of every day in every way. Centuries earlier God had set down a requirement that all first-born males were to be consecrated to Him. Parents would bring that child to the temple and make a sacrifice in keeping with that expectation. It was a full recognition that this child, like all else in life, belonged totally to the Lord.

There is a vital truth here for all believers. Following Jesus means far more than accepting Him as personal Savior as a way of escape. The choice to follow Christ is a dedication of all of life to Him. Becoming a Christian is an act of total consecration that impacts a person spiritually, emotionally, psychologically, relationally, vocationally, economically, and behaviorally. It is an invitation to surrender to His complete Lordship. Granted, it takes time even to begin to understand what all that means. But from the beginning of the journey, even the newest follower should be aware that the path of total consecration stands before him. The idea that a person can receive Jesus as Savior and move on in life as it was before is not biblical. Jesus is Lord and the deepest level of commitment will be required of all who choose to follow.

Jesus' dedication in the Temple was also not a private matter. Certainly the deepest impact would have been upon the hearts of Mary and Joseph, yet many others were there that day. We already know from the story that Simeon and Anna were present, but undoubtedly others were as well. The Temple was open to all the people of God and every day many would come and go. Some would arrive for seasons of prayer, others to make the required sacrifices. It was a busy and very public place. And it was in that public setting that Mary and Joseph dedicated Jesus before the Lord.

I believe such an act of public consecration is vital to the Christian experience. In some way new believers should have the opportunity to stand before the community of Christ and declare their dedication to the Lordship of Jesus. Traditions vary as to how this happens within the church. For some, this takes place at baptism, when the new believer makes a public declaration of repentance, belief, and dedication to Christ. In other contexts this happens when the new believer is received into church membership. He or she makes a statement of faith and a vow of dedication before the people. And in turn the community of Christians promises to support on the journey. I have often been moved when new Christians have the opportunity to testify of how they turned to Jesus and the difference He has made in their lives. Standing before a group of people is in itself not easy and reveals a serious level of commitment in a person's life.

Regardless of the method, public dedication to the Lordship of Christ is essential to the Christian experience. It openly signifies that this person is now surrendering to Christ and allowing Him access to all of his or her life. The public context for this dedication takes the promise of consecration to a deeper level for the new believer. It also welcomes accountability and support from the community of Christ, which is critical to the journey. No one expects the person to follow flawlessly or be an immediate saint. Everyone recognizes that a person will move closer to Christ as the journey progresses and grow as a believer. But the act of dedication is a consecration of the heart. The person who publicly stands to declare herself before the Lord and His people is signifying that her deepest, most passionate desire is to belong totally to Christ. The path has been chosen.

Jesus also received very specific blessings at his dedication. When Simeon saw the child, he was quickened by the Spirit, and told by God that the baby in Mary's arms was the prophesied Messiah. The Lord had promised Simeon that he would see that day, and it had finally arrived, suddenly and wonderfully. Simeon was so moved by the experience that he took Jesus in his arms and began to speak blessings to

God over the Christ child and to Mary and Joseph. There was prophetic power in his words, invoking the presence of God upon Jesus and his future ministry.

Christians have the power to bless, an authority that is modeled in scripture and given by the Lord. When spoken with faith, words of blessing can invite spiritual empowerment upon people that will impact their lives significantly. I have taught and practiced this for years and can testify that spoken blessings do have power. I pastored a congregation where this was a regular part of our community life. Whenever a person

Christians have the power to bless, an authority that is modeled in scripture and given by the Lord.

came for prayer, the person praying would wait upon the Spirit to shape a blessing to be spoken over the individual. Many times I have heard people say that receiving the blessing was the most moving part of the time in prayer.

I believe this practice should happen particularly when new believers are standing to declare faith and dedication to the Lord. In response to this heartfelt commitment, the community of Jesus should speak words of blessings over the person. These should be motivated by the Holy Spirit and delivered with confidence. I am suggesting that it involves more than "I pray that the Lord blesses you." Mature Christians should exercise the authority given to them in Christ and pronounce blessings that flow from God's heart and Word. When delivering a blessing we can lay hands on the new believer as an act of impartation. When I have seen this happen, people are deeply affected. Many times individuals approached me later and asked for the specific words I spoke, because they held such meaning and hope for them.

Finally, the act of public dedication and blessing should be an occasion for great praise and celebration. Simeon and Anna came alive with thanks at the dedication of Jesus, and broke forth in spontaneous praise to God. The Bible says that when Anna saw Jesus she gave praise to God and told people everywhere about Jesus (Luke 2:38). What a marvelous example to everyone! The plan of redemption is all about God's goodness and love displayed in the coming of Jesus Christ.

When new believers—or Christians of any age, for that matter—stand to dedicate themselves to the Lord, the community of Christ should respond with glorious praise to God. Such moments of consecration impact all who are present, reminding them of God's gift of eternal life through Christ and the invitation to intimacy with the Lord. People often recall their own experience of new birth and remember when they declared their own commitment to the Lord. People praise God for the new brothers and sisters who are being dedicated, as well as give thanks for the community of Christ that stands to rededicate itself to one another. Such moments bring to life the words of Hebrews 13:15, "Through Jesus therefore, let us continually offer to God a sacrifice of praise, the fruit of lips that confess his name."

A Crossroad to Choose

The time will come on the Christian journey when people must decide to move beyond private belief and publicly dedicate themselves to the Lord in the community of Christ. Many will try to convince people that receiving Jesus as Savior is enough. They will claim that this decision opens the door to the born again experience that is necessary to eternal life. Some people seem to believe that God offers the less committed a ticket to heaven, a "get out of hell card" for all who at least accept Jesus. This is a cheap misrepresentation of the gospel. It is a path of least resistance and it leads to a hollow Christianity.

The promise of Christ is much more than a place in heaven. It is an invitation to be in intimate fellowship with Him, to be secure in His love, transformed into His likeness, and empowered to take part in changing the world. The way of Christ demands a heart fully consecrated to God, inviting His Lordship over every area of life. Dedication of this level will not be possible in human strength alone. But the presence of Jesus on the path, the indwelling of the Holy Spirit within, and the support of the community of Christ makes it a consecration that will be life changing.

The act of public dedication is an act of faith and obedience for believers. It is also a great privilege for all who choose to follow Christ. They stand before the church present and the church in heaven, consecrating all that they are to the plan and purpose of God. It is a public declaration that invites one and all to know that Jesus is their Lord. This was the way of Jesus, and it is the path all Christians will be challenged to take. Jesus, the One who gave all for believers, stands at the crossroads. He beckons those who are willing to come, follow wholeheartedly, surrender completely, and walk with Him publicly and privately as the Lord of life.

5 / Confrontation

Satan does not play fair. Ever. He is constantly at war with God and His people and he follows no rules of engagement when in battle. He shows no compassion to the wounded, never gives quarter, and does not voluntarily return prisoners of war. He will violently assault any person, anywhere, anytime, regardless of age or station in life. The evil one is driven by hate for all that is good and works to strike at people when they are most vulnerable. He despises the image of God within people and absolutely abhors the Spirit of God that abides within Christians. Satan is full of darkness and works to make every living person a victim of his hideous schemes. With him are minions of spirits that have been cast from the presence of God, demons hell bent on destruction and violence to God's creation.

Jesus called the evil one a thief and said that he came to steal, kill, and destroy (John 10:10). Scripture has referred to him in a variety of ways, including the ruler of this world (I John 5:18,19), the prince of the power of the air (Eph. 2:2, KJV), an angel of light (II Cor. 11:14), a roaring lion (I Pet.

5:8), the slanderer (I Tim. 5:14), and the accuser (Rev. 12:10). Each title represents some aspect of his evil activity and is given in scripture to equip Christians to stand against him. He constantly works in both subtle and overt ways to lead people into bondage and ultimate eternal destruction. He is no myth, he plays no games, and the battle is all too real.

But there is good news. Jesus defeated the evil one at

Satan constantly works to lead people into bondage and ultimate eternal destruction.

Calvary. As a result, Christians are not helpless victims who have no hope against the devil and his schemes. Jesus Christ made a public display of the dark forces when He triumphed over them at the cross (Col. 2:13-15). He died on Calvary to destroy the very one who held the power of death over people, the devil (Heb. 2:14). Christians can have confidence that, though the evil one is real, the presence of Christ within empowers them to be overcomers (I John 4:4). And believers can rest secure in the battle knowing that the Lord is committed to strengthen and protect them (II Thess. 3:3), and ultimately bring them safe into God's heavenly kingdom (II Tim. 4:18). In the final day, Satan and all that is evil will be thrown into the lake of fire and tormented throughout eternity for the havoc and destruction they have brought to humankind (Rev. 20:7-15).

The Battle Continues

Christians must understand that, while Jesus has won the victory, Satan remains active warring against God and His people. The Bible says that when the time of Christ's coming nears, he will begin to attack with even more vehemence and violence (Rev. 12:12). Those who have walked with Christ for even a short time know that he is not a figment of someone's overactive imagination. He is the force behind everything that is wrong in this world and will work violently if necessary to stamp out even the slightest glimmer of light in a person's life.

No Christian is free from Satan's designs. It does not matter whether that person is a spiritual giant who has walked with Christ for decades, or a newborn Christian who has only known the Lord for a matter of minutes. Nowhere is this more evident than in the story of Christ and His birth.

From Joy to Sadness

The news surrounding Christ's birth must have spread quickly around Bethlehem. The angelic visitation to the shepherds, and the announcement that the Anointed One of God had been born, must have stirred a storm of activity among the local residents. It had been centuries since any such direct revelation from God had occurred. That alone marked a new day for God's people. But the announcement must have seemed too good to believe. The Christ had been born, in a manger in Bethlehem! That message was, for the Jews, the fulfillment of a hope that was centuries old.

The Israelite people had experienced a long history of oppression. They had been the slaves of Egyptians, exploited by Assyrians, taken into bondage by Babylonians, ravaged by Greeks, and, at the time of Christ's birth, oppressed by a Roman occupation force.

The local residents had personally experienced the heavy hand of their captors. Their crops were pillaged, money was taken from them in unfair taxation, and they were obliged to serve any Roman at will. Their religion was ridiculed, their women abused, and their children terrorized. Many of their countrymen had become collaborators, joining the Romans in making money off their own people. The first century was a time of great sadness and oppression for God's people, and many began to lose heart. Would a day of deliverance ever come from God?

Into this darkness came the Light. The Christ-child was the hope of many generations, and finally, at least to the residents of Bethlehem, it seemed that He had arrived. The long-awaited Messiah had come to re-establish the throne of David and begin a kingdom that would last forever. The star did shine, the angels did sing, and the baby was born. It simply had to be true. In their minds, the coming of God's Anointed One meant the overthrow of all oppressors and a return to the golden years of Davidic reign. The people must have been excited. They could probably be seen whispering to each other, out of the hearing of their oppressors, that the day of deliverance was at hand.

I wonder what they began to think about, dream about, envision for their future? They may have talked about the day when there would be no occupying army to take their best crops, press them into service, and tax them unfairly. It could be that they dreamed about the freedom to go anywhere they wanted, when they wanted. They might have imagined walking the streets without fear, talking openly with friends and neighbors, sleeping soundly without thoughts of a Roman squad taking a loved one away bearing a cross. Most likely they felt a new joy begin to settle in to their hearts, fueled by hopes that the light of God was about to shine upon them once again.

But suddenly black darkness fell upon the land. Herod had heard about the birth of Jesus and was told that the child in Bethlehem was the king that scripture had foretold. This threatened Herod so he plotted to find the child through the magi and destroy him. But the magi outwitted Herod and went home by another route, avoiding any contact with him. An angel warned Joseph and Mary that their child's life was in danger and instructed them to flee to Egypt. Immediately they escaped south with Jesus. Herod, not knowing that they were no longer in Bethlehem, determined to eliminate Jesus no matter the cost.

Herod dispatched soldiers to the small town of Bethlehem with orders to kill every boy who was two years old and under. His despicable actions were driven by more than personal insecurity. They were empowered by the forces of evil determined to stamp out the light of God's love. And the small town that had recently been alive with hope fell into darkest despair. Every precious boy child was brutally murdered. People who had for the first time dreamed of new life were left grieving, battling an emptiness beyond description. The promise of deliverance suddenly turned to an apparent death sentence.

Given the size of Bethlehem at the time, few people in the community were left untouched. The angels were not singing, the star was not shining, and the children were dead. The weeping could be heard throughout the land as the undefended and vulnerable had been savagely destroyed. Satan had been ruthless, venting his full rage against God's mission of love. The people who had gone to the mountaintop of promise felt that they had been driven to the valley of death. But regardless of how it seemed to the people, the day was not lost and Jesus was still alive. He had been saved to fulfill the promise of salvation. He lived on in order to die on His own terms, as the atoning sacrifice for all people. And He rose again and reigns to this day at the right hand of God Almighty.

A Lesson to be Learned

One of the most important lessons to be learned from this story concerns those who are new in the Christian faith. Satan does not reserve his schemes for those who have walked with Christ for many years. He is a master at trying to stamp out the light of Christ before it has the opportunity to grow into a mighty flame. He hits hardest when people are weak and vulnerable. And so he regularly targets newborn believers.

My experience in the first days and weeks of faith parallels, to a far lesser degree, the dynamics of the story just reviewed. When I first came to Christ I was alive like I had never been before. I felt free, cleansed of sin, and walking without the heavy load of guilt that I had carried for so long. Scripture was alive when I read it and I felt that I had an open line to God in prayer. And I sensed the presence of the Holy Spirit in my life. I wanted to go to church as much as possible and was thrilled that old desires had faded away. It seemed that everything was going great for me, and I attributed it all to my new relationship with Jesus.

But things began to change—for the worse. I found that the desire to slip back into old, sinful behaviors grew with unreasonable intensity. I had naively thought that my previous struggles with things like sexual sin, aggressive behavior, and self-centered living were long gone. But the temptation to turn back to sin had suddenly become overwhelming. I felt as if I was being torn apart inside by two powerful forces, each pulling me in opposite directions. On one side was the newfound presence of love, gently yet powerfully drawing me to the place of freedom. But on the other was the lure of past pleasures, a dark force that seemed to have gained strength and threatened to undo my new life in Christ.

And I fell, more than once. It was not so easy saying no to sin, and guilt began to weigh upon me once again. And it somehow seemed that there were more than a few reasons to stay home on Sunday and just sleep. I began to spin, wondering what had happened to my new-born relationship with the Lord. Soon I was discouraged and wondered if I had really experienced the transformation that I had testified to just days before. I found it difficult to pray, wrestled again with feelings of shame, and wanted to avoid my new Christian friends like the plague. I began to question the reality of the

---

New Christians must not give up, for Satan has no real power to destroy the light that the Spirit has ignited in believing hearts.

---

entire experience. Had something genuinely happened to me when I accepted Christ, or was it all just a temporary emotional high?

I became discouraged and seriously considered turning my back on the whole thing. It seemed I was a total failure at being a Christian. If I had really given my life to Christ I would not have been caving into temptation and doubting the Lord. Or at least so I thought. I did not realize that I was a victim of Satan's scheme to stamp out the light of Christ within my heart. He had determined to attack me savagely in my spiritual infancy, hoping to destroy my newfound relationship with the Lord.

What was occurring in my life was happening because I was a new creation in Christ. I felt totally abnormal, when in fact this is the way the evil one has worked for centuries. I wanted to blame myself for all my obvious weaknesses and failings. The truth is the evil one was bearing down to destroy what God had started in my life. Thankfully, the Lord preserved me and I was able to move on along the journey with Christ and discover more about the realities of spiritual warfare. As I grew I learned about the strategies of evil and how to stand in the victory of Jesus Christ. It would have helped in the first days of faith to know that such battles are a normal part of the journey. It would have encouraged me to hold on to Christ as He was holding on to me.

Facing the Crossroads

I cannot predict when, but there will be times when the evil one will attack. I am confident that this will begin to happen soon after a person is born again of the Holy Spirit. The evil one hates the Light and particularly sets strategies aimed at bringing down people during spiritual infancy, just as he tried with the baby Jesus. Almost as soon as new freedom comes, the darkness will press in to destroy. New Christians should know this from the very beginning.

Temptation will be overwhelming at times, trials will be great, doubts will come, and there will be very discouraging days. Many will feel as if they have fallen from the mountaintop to the valley of despair. This does not happen because new Christians are especially weak and sinful. It is the strategy of Satan to oppress new believers and turn them away from the path of Jesus.

After determining to follow Christ and grow close to Him, people will face great trial. Voices will try to discourage and disqualify with the lie that they have no right to keep walking with Christ. This is a tactic of the evil one that is as old as time itself. New Christians must not give up, for Satan has no real power to destroy the light that the Holy Spirit has ignited in believing hearts. God's word tells Christians to resist the devil (James 4:7), and move forward with Christ. When the evil one stands against the upward path and roars like a lion, new Christians as well as old are to stand against him, trusting that God will bring deliverance (I Pet. 5:9). And always, believers are to call out to Jesus, who will faithfully strengthen and protect them from Satan (II Thess. 3:3). These promises of God are sure.

All Christians, regardless of how long they have been in the faith, should be part of a loving community. The family of God is in place to encourage people to stay the path, for it is the only way to truly grow intimate with the Lord and be healed. The community is to urge people to move past the threats into the strong arms of the One who loves them all. The community of Christ is called to protect the young in the Lord, surround the weak against evil schemes, and together fight the good fight of faith.

Later in our discussion we will learn how to face the enemy and overcome him as Jesus did in the desert. Here, from the story of Jesus' early life, we have learned that the path of faith involves confrontation with darkness. Christians will face these times, not because they do not believe right, behave correctly, or serve adequately. They come because they belong to the Lord and walk with Him. They must not look to find an easier way. Jesus walked this path and now invites all to follow. He is faithful and will carry us through to a new and spacious place of love, intimacy, and life.

6 / *Construction*

Iworked as a carpenter during college and part of seminary. Actually, I began learning about construction in high school, when a neighbor gave me a job on a crew that built new homes. At first I was the gopher for the skilled workers. But by the time I entered college I had learned enough to qualify as a full-fledged carpenter. I thoroughly enjoyed that kind of work and still take on small jobs that require my hammer and power saw. There is something special about building. Part of what I love about it is that, at the end of the day, I can see what I have done. All the hard work actually creates something useful.

I learned a great deal about life by doing construction work. Especially important was a lesson taught to me on a warm January day in 1975. I was in seminary at the time and newly married. I tried to stay busy working construction whenever I was not in class. That fall the weather had been especially frigid, and it was hard for the bricklayers to lay block for foundations. Below zero concrete freezes, which kept the foundation workers from doing their job. Eventually we had no new foundation upon which to build a house, and so we were all unemployed for several weeks.

Finally the temperature warmed long enough for the bricklayers to quickly put up some block. But no sooner had they finished than the weather turned and we faced a long spell below freezing. Except for a little discomfort, that does not really affect carpenters. For weeks we worked framing the two-story home. We laid floors, raised walls, put partitions in place, built basement stairs, and set windows. The majority of the rough carpentry was complete, except for finishing the roof.

Then came that important January day. Several of us were on the roof nailing shingles, putting up trim, and placing flashing around the chimney. It was unseasonably warm, and wonderful. It felt great to have the sun on my back after such cold weather. All of a sudden, late in the day, there was a low rumble. The house began to move slowly toward one side, followed by a sudden tilt and jerk. It was dramatic enough to send tools sliding off the roof, and men grabbing for something secure. It felt like a small earthquake, but we knew that was not the cause.

We all made our way down from the roof. Looking inside we saw that windows had broken, stairs were out of place, and walls were far out of level. We knew that this all would need to be fixed, but it was not the problem that caused the destruction. Not until we made our way to the basement did we see what had happened. An entire side of the foundation had given way.

At first the whole thing was puzzling. How could a concrete wall just collapse? But with closer inspection everything became clear. Weeks earlier, when the foundation had been laid, it had not had time to set up. The cement had actually frozen, giving it the appearance of being ready to build upon. We had unknowingly been constructing a home on a "green" foundation. And on that warm day, the frozen concrete began to thaw. The pressure from the house above and the landfill pressing at the base was too much for it to bear. Finally, the foundation gave way.

More than a little damage had been done to the house. Our haste to get back to work had compromised the project, and in the end it cost far more time and money than neces-

---

Jesus spent years in preparation before moving into the great demands of public ministry.

---

sary to finish the two-story home. I learned that day that foundations might be unglamorous and unseen, but they are critical to sound construction. Few people will ever visit a beautiful home and ask to see the gray block and mortar. But if patient care is not taken to see that the foundation is secure before building, trouble will follow sooner or later.

A Metaphor of Life

I believe this story provides a perfect metaphor for what happens to many people on the Christian journey. For years there has been a great emphasis upon being busy in the Lord's work. From the first day of faith I heard about a lost and broken world and the importance of giving my all for the kingdom. The church I attended was always listing opportunities for jobs in the church and soon after coming to Christ I was enlisted in some "critical" task. I set about doing all I could for the Lord. Wholehearted service was a standard of commitment for one and all to embrace. I learned this all too well, resulting in my own lengthy season of burnout.

There seems to be an alarming rate of breakdown in the faith these days. Many people begin ministry like a bright and shining star, only to burn out across the galaxy of the church, never to be seen or heard from again. I have watched this happen to many Christians, including "celebrities" who suddenly find the Lord. These well known, yet new believers, are often immediately placed in positions of pressure and responsibility, speaking about their conversion within weeks of coming to Christ. It seems that their names and faces are everywhere for a while, and then, suddenly, they are gone. Why? What happens?

I sat in a friend's living room one evening talking with a nationally known comedian who had become a well-known Christian celebrity. He had gone from unbeliever to Christian poster child in the blink of an eye. Organizations were pushing him out front to attract crowds and dollars. He was told that this was important for the kingdom and his schedule was filled with appointments to give his testimony. But in time, just like the house built on a "green" foundation, everything began to give. What people saw looked and sounded great. But the people around him had not taken care to see that he had secured the foundation of his life. And under all the pressure it all caved in on him.

Thankfully, my friend, a well-known Christian leader, came alongside and helped him put the pieces back together. His hidden life was receiving the attention needed to make the public life healthy and effective. This is a lesson many in the church need to learn. And as always, Jesus is the very best teacher.

Construction

If urgency is the central factor that motivates some churches and Christian leaders to press people into service soon after coming to Christ, what do they do with Jesus? Why did He wait until age thirty to launch His public ministry? I am convinced that it is because constructing a secure foundation was critical to the Lord's life and mission on earth. Little is known beyond legend about the hidden years of Jesus. Scripture is silent from age twelve to about thirty, except for the fact that Jesus had spent that time at home with his family, serving as a carpenter like his father. The one clue we do have about this period in the Lord's life comes in Luke 2:52. It is the last statement made before the silent years begin. "And Jesus grew in wisdom and stature, and in favor with God and men."

These years may be hidden, but they certainly were not wasted. Jesus was securing the foundation of His life. The Bible says that He grew in wisdom during that time, which tells the reader that He was learning far more than knowledge. He was gaining understanding, which is essential if one wants to respond to life in a healthy, mature way. Scripture says that He grew in stature, which implies more than physical maturity and strength. And God's word tells the reader that Jesus grew in favor with God and men. This is the critical relational component of life, where Jesus grew to experience intimacy with His Heavenly Father and the people with whom he lived and related. Many today would say that being mature in wisdom, strength, and relational skills is the key to personal well-being and effectiveness in life. Somehow Jesus must have known that thousands of years before the behavioralists discovered it!

How did this happen in Christ's life? Granted, anything I suggest is mere conjecture. But it would not be too much of a stretch to say that it did not occur through academic pursuit. I believe Jesus allowed life to be His teacher. Through observation, inquiry, and experience, Jesus grew. Every day was an opportunity and every situation a lesson for life. Undoubtedly the presence of the Holy Spirit was a key factor in Jesus'

development, drawing Him to the spiritual realities of kingdom living.

Some may reject the very thought that Jesus, the Son of
God, needed instruction at all. But that objection is based on
an inaccurate understanding of the incarnation. Jesus came to
earth and walked life as a human, not as God. Yes he was
God, but He set aside His divine powers to experience the
path humans walk. His process of personal development was
no more or less vital than any one else who has walked this
earth. And we see from His life that it was important enough
for Him to spend years in preparation before moving into the
great demands of public ministry. Constructing a secure foundation is important work and worth the time it takes.

The Apostle Paul had a similar season of development
and preparation after he was converted. At first, he seemed to
be popular on the speaking circuit, telling people about his
Damascus Road experience. I am sure that the one who had
persecuted Christians but was now following Christ could
draw a good crowd. But after a short while, and under great
pressure, Paul entered a season of seclusion and growth. It
lasted between fourteen and seventeen years and, given his
impact on the world, seems to have been time well spent. I
have read of many Christian leaders who had such seasons
of silence and growth, and I have yet to hear that any of
them regretted the experience. I once heard Billy Graham
say that if he had it to do all over again, he would spend far
more time in preparation and prayer. That is a model of
Christian leadership we desperately need today. It is a commitment to necessary construction.

Facing A Crossroads

Christians cannot afford to miss this crossroads with Jesus.
Granted there will be many who speak otherwise. New
believers will be told that the time is short and the need is

great. Pleas will be made to do everything possible as soon as possible for the cause of the kingdom. And I am sure some will hear the oft-made comment that "it is better to burn out for the Lord than rust out." Pressure and guilt will be applied to get believers "up front and out there for the Lord." But that is the wrong path to take. It leads to unnecessary pain and waste, and the casualties along the way are innumerable.

Christ's cause is great and important. But new believers should place high value on the hidden work of growing strong. Jesus did not hesitate to walk that way, and neither should we. The better the foundation, the larger the house a person can build. I cannot predict how long the season of construction will take. It is different for everyone. But I can point to some foundational experiences and understandings that should be prioritized during this time.

Experience leads me to prioritize four things during the hidden season of construction. First, a new Christian should grow in God's love. It is high and wide and deep, and able to transform lives like nothing else. Time with the Lord and time with His loving community is the best way for this to happen. Many Christians are compromised because they serve God without knowing the wonder of His incomparable love. It is the block and mortar of Christian experience.

Second, a new Christian must be established in his or her new identity. The world assaults people's self-worth daily. Our society promotes the idea that love and acceptance come only to the beautiful, wealthy, powerful and successful. Desperate for acceptance, many people pursue these ideals relentlessly, only to find them deeply unsatisfying. Others live with the constant despair of not measuring up in such world. Nothing could be further from the truth for God's children. New believers must know that they are new creations in Christ Jesus and be secure in their identity as children of God.

Third, the season of construction should be a time for healing deep emotional wounds. Most people come to faith beat up inside and trapped in dysfunctional behaviors. Left unaddressed these weaknesses will lead to great pain. Constructing a foundation is a time for filling in the cracks, and in this case, the sealant is healing love. God cares about emotional pain and has made a provision for freedom through Christ.

Finally, new believers should learn to pray effectively. There is transformational power in deep prayer. It draws one into a flow of God's presence that can move mountains. Such prayer is alive and dynamic, strengthening the believer to move forward in the power of Jesus Christ.

I would also emphasize that the new believer read Scripture and learn basic Christian doctrine. But once again, I would encourage the new believer to remember that doing this should be relationally focused, not academically driven. People should allow God's word and truth to draw them ever closer to Him, not just provide them with facts and information.

A time of service and sacrificial ministry lies ahead for every Christian. Participation will be demanding and vital to the kingdom cause. It will not be easy and the pressure will be great. Now is the time for the hidden work, the foundational work that is critical to that day. Very soon the Christian will hear his or her own personal call to follow Jesus into servant ministry. But here, at this crossroads, we are invited to say yes to construction. The Lord has shown the way, and wants all that are His to follow. Wisdom will respond and allow the work to be done. Few will see what is happening, for it is normally hidden. But when the time to build arrives they will sense the security that comes from so firm a foundation.

7 / *Commission*

When Jesus stepped onto the stage of human history as an adult He did not question His purpose for being there. He had heard the call of God and was confident to move forward and fulfill His assignment. Life held incredible meaning for Jesus. The hidden years had prepared Him well, and now the time had come for Jesus to be about His Father's business. Beginning with His baptism and carrying on until the ascension, Christ was single-minded about His purpose.

Some, including members of His own family, doubted what Jesus was about, thinking He had lost His mind. Some people tried to dissuade Him, more than a few worked to distract Him, others made every effort to ruin Him, several key people deserted Him, a close friend betrayed Him, and in the end forces aligned to destroy Him. But Jesus kept His vision clear and prevailed against them all. He knew that He was on a mission from God.

The commission that Jesus received was well defined and He regularly communicated it to all who came close enough to hear His message. He knew that He had been sent from above (John 6:57; 7:16, 28, 29; 8:29), to preach the gospel of the kingdom (Mark 1:14,15, 38), and that He would give His life (John 3:16; 10:14) to save the world (John 3:16; Luke 19:10). He saw Himself as the light of the world (John 8:12), the truth and the way (John 14:6), and the resurrection and the life (John 11:25). He never backed away from these claims, even when they cost Him his life. Jesus moved forward in life with a clear sense of His divinely ordained destiny.

Jesus experienced joy on the journey, but there was also a great deal of trial and difficulty. He faced spiritual opposition regularly, as well as great misunderstanding from the political and religious communities of His day. There was rumor and rejection at every turn. But Jesus pressed on with authority and power. His followers were not always the brightest lights on the tree, but He invested deeply in them and moved forward to touch a broken and hurting world with them at His side. Even the agony of Gethsemane did not cause Jesus to turn aside into another path. He was surrendered to God and knew from the beginning that the road led to Jerusalem, and from there to a hill called Golgotha. Like a lamb going to slaughter, He was silent. Jesus knew that it was all part of the plan, and He had said yes. He was a man with a call on His life.

Hearing the Call of God

Jesus appeared to his disciples several times after His resurrection from the dead. On one occasion they were meeting behind a locked door. John recorded the event in his gospel:

> On the evening of the first day of the week, when the disciples were together, with the doors locked for fear of the Jews, Jesus came and stood among them and said, "Peace be with you!" After he said this, he showed them his hands and side. The disciples were

overjoyed when they saw the Lord.

Again Jesus said to, "Peace be with you." As the Father has sent me, I am sending you. With that he breathed on them and said, "Receive the Holy Spirit. If you forgive anyone his sins they will be forgiven; if you do not forgive them they are not forgiven." (John 20:19-22)

This passage identifies the general call that Christians have upon their lives. Jesus has commissioned Christians to carry on His ministry. What He began, we are left to finish in the power

---

Jesus has commissioned Christians to carry on His ministry. What He began, we are left to finish in the power of His name.

---

of His name. No believer is left out, no Christian exempt. As Jesus was sent into the world, so all Christians have now been sent into the world. Some are to go to their families and friends, others to people they do not even know.

Most Christians will serve Christ in their own hometown, while others will travel to far away places in response to His command. Granted people need preparation, and the opportunity to grow and strengthen for the task. But with that in mind, let this much be clear: we are people under orders. We have a commission from Jesus Christ to bring hope and healing to the world.

The distinction between lay and professional ministry has hurt the church. It has given the false impression that some special people have been called of God to spend their lives in ministry, while the rest go about life as normal. It has also caused some dear people to think that they are second-class citizens, unable to really serve the Lord. It has provided others with a license to stay uninvolved. This is tragic, for the words of Jesus give all an opportunity to make their life count, as well as present an obligation for His people to fulfill His command.

The dear people I went to serve as pastor in 1975 believed that they were hiring me to do all the ministry in their church. They had the idea that they would simply support me with dollars and prayers. It was not easy convincing them that the church was really a family where everyone served the cause of Christ. My situation was not unique. Since then I have met countless pastors who have gone into local churches were people live under that same misguided notion. That is unfortunate. The path of ministry is a great privilege and opportunity for all who become Christ's disciples. This needs to happen as people have had opportunity to grow and become secure in the love of God.

Unity and Diversity

It is important that believers recognize that we are all ministers of Christ. Some people, like myself, serve the Lord by working for Christian organizations where time is spent in activities that are directly related to Christian ministry. Pastors have ministries like that, as do evangelists, teachers, missionaries and Christian counselors. Their vocations provide daily opportunities to do kingdom work.

But the majority of Christian ministers serve in secular jobs, where they daily have the opportunity to fulfill Christ's command. They may be doctors, nurses, bank clerks, factory workers, schoolteachers, homemakers, students or bus drivers. While the work they perform does not always seem directly related to ministry, the context provides an opportunity to serve people as they serve the Lord. Unfortunately many believers do not see it this way. They believe that a "call" to ministry only happens to those who are in professional Christian service. All Christians are commissioned by Christ and should see their context of life and employment as the primary place where that call is fulfilled.

While we are all called, each individual believer is placed in ministry and equipped for service in his or her unique way. The Apostle Paul explains this best in I Corinthians 12, where he uses the human body as a metaphor for the church. He emphasized that there is only one body of Christ, which is the church. This church is His body on earth, doing what He would do if He were still here. And this one body, the church, receives its orders from its head, Jesus Christ. The body cannot go off on its own and do as it pleases. It must submit to Christ, for he is in charge.

Paul also emphasized diversity in I Corinthians 12. He said that the body of Christ is made up of many different parts, just like the human body. In this case the parts are people, placed in the body according to God's will. People are to serve as the hands and legs, eyes and ears of the Lord, all working together to fulfill the Lord's commands. No part of the body is more important than the other. Each is doing a different but essential part in being the body of Jesus on earth. If a member of Christ's body decides not to do its part, then the body is handicapped and will not be able to function in the world as it could. The body is to work in harmony if it wants to fulfill the commands of the Lord effectively. There must be unity, while accepting and celebrating diversity.

Spiritual Gifts

But how does a member of Christ's body know what part he or she is to play? How does a person determine the specific call upon his or her life? These are critical questions and

Paul anticipated them in chapter twelve. He said that the Holy Spirit gives all Christians spiritual gifts. These gifts are to be discovered by each believer, developed, and then used within the body to fulfill the commission of the Lord. A spiritual gift is a special ability that God gives a person for use in the body of Christ. These gifts are empowered by the Holy Spirit, enabling the person to serve in ways beyond their normal human ability. Those who discern their spiritual gifts need to then spend time growing in them so that they will be effective in these God-given abilities. The Bible mentions many different spiritual gifts, including the following:

I Corinthians 12
Wisdom
Knowledge
Faith
Healings
Miracles
Prophecy
Discernment
Tongues,
Interpretation of Tongues
Prophets
Teachers
Administration

Ephesians 4
Apostles
Pastor
Evangelist
Teacher

Romans 12
Prophesying
Serving

Teaching
Encouraging
Contributing
Leadership
Mercy

This list is not exclusive, just illustrative of all that God does through the Holy Spirit in the lives of His people.

I constantly meet people who struggle with their self-image and sense of purpose. That is a difficult battle to face

---

Each individual believer is placed in ministry and equipped for service in his or her unique way.

---

and is often complicated by feelings of inadequacy and insecurity. God's Word addresses that problem head on when it teaches people that they are vital to God's plan for the world and spiritually gifted to fulfill the commission of the Lord. God has placed treasures of the Spirit inside every believing person. Christians are challenged to go on an internal treasure hunt of self-discovery and celebrate all that God has placed within them. Some believers may not know their purpose, but God does, and it relates directly to the commission of Christ and the gifts that the Spirit has given to them.

It will take time for believers to discover their gifts and then grow in them. They will need to study them with other Christians and pray about which gifts may be present within them. But this effort should be exciting to Christians, strengthening the conviction that God has made them unique for a very special purpose and plan. The gifts that God gives people will be used in a variety of different ways, and in innumerable and varied contexts. Some Christians will serve in churches, others in institutions and para-church ministries. Many believers will find that God calls them to use their gifts among families and friends, while others will serve God in secular contexts. There is rich unity and diversity in the body. All Christians are commissioned by Christ and equipped to serve the Lord, but every person and situation will be different.

Facing A Crossroads

It has often been said that the church is like a football game. Hundreds of people in the stands desperately needing exercise are watching twenty-two people on the field who desperately need rest. There is some truth to this statement. In the church there is a tension between two extremes. One group is pushing hard to get believers active in ministry and set them to task long before they are ready. This results in burnout and bitterness and causes more damage than it is worth.

But there is an unhealthy inertia on the other side that relegates serving the Lord to those who are called to full-time ministry. There is a tragic lack of understanding about the commission that Jesus has given to His church. We are all ministers of Christ, full time. Though there are different gifts and callings, every believer is part of the plan. We are to spend our lives participating in the mission of redemption that Jesus gave His life to provide. It is the privilege and responsibility of all who claim to follow Christ. Jesus made his choice clear when on earth. His life belonged to God and His days were spent obediently fulfilling His appointed mission. Every Christian will come to the crossroad where that same issue must be personally decided.

There is, as always, a way of least resistance. A Christian can take the path that leads to inactivity, an easy journey to a sad brand of Christian consumerism that allows people to sit back and watch. It is a draining experience that weakens the individual's faith, reducing it into impotency. Those who choose that way end up disillusioned, eventually determining that religion really doesn't make much difference after all.

But there is the path that Jesus took in life and it leads to sacrificial ministry to a lost and broken world. At this point in the journey Jesus does not invite, He commands. Believers are summoned to His side where they hear the word, "So send I you." The possibilities are both exciting and frightening. Those who dare to consider following Christ's command wonder what they could ever do to make a difference. They see what it cost Jesus and question whether they have what it takes to follow. In that moment, when the heart is yearning to obey but the will is weak and hesitant, Jesus acts. He breathes upon His own and says, "Receive the Holy Spirit." It is the time to journey on.

8 / Credentialing

Jesus received the anointing of the Holy Spirit before He took one step toward public ministry. Those who are wise will follow that same path.

The life of Jesus on earth was intricately linked to the person and work of the Holy Spirit. This can be seen in scripture from the conception to the ascension of Jesus, indicating that true ministry is done in partnership with "the Flame of Love." An important moment in the partnership between Christ and the Spirit came at His baptism (Matt. 3:1-16). John the Baptist, cousin of Jesus, had spoken of the coming Christ. He told people that he was but a forerunner, a voice crying out in the desert to prepare the way. John told people that the Christ would come and baptize them with the fire of the Holy Spirit.

When Jesus came to John at the Jordan, he asked John to baptize Him, but John was hesitant. But Jesus said that this baptism must happen, and so John consented. When Jesus came up out of the water, the Holy Spirit descended upon Him like a dove, and God spoke, saying, "This is my beloved Son, whom I love; with him I am well pleased." This double blessing sealed within Christ two essential realities critical to the ministry He was now to begin. God was absolutely in love with Him and full of Fatherly pride. Jesus could be sure of that. And the Holy Spirit had filled and anointed Him to do the ministry set before Him in supernatural kingdom power.

Three things stand out about the ministry of Jesus and the person of the Holy Spirit. First, Jesus submitted to the Spirit's leading. Immediately after His baptism, Jesus was led into the wilderness by the Holy Spirit. There He faced the temptation of the evil one and returned to Galilee under the Spirit's power (Luke 4:1-14). Second, Jesus ministered to people with incredible power. He turned water into wine (John 2:1-11), healed the sick (Mark 1:29-34), cast out demons (Luke 8:26-39), fed five thousand with five loaves and two fish (Mark 6:30-44), walked on water (Matt. 14:22-36), stilled storms (Mark 4:35-41), and raised the dead (Mark 5:35-43).

These displays of supernatural power served to defeat the evil one, free the afflicted and oppressed, and identify Jesus as legitimately sent by God. When Jesus stood to read the scroll in the Temple at the inauguration of His ministry, He read these words from Isaiah: "The Spirit of the Lord is upon me because he has anointed me to preach good news to the poor. He has sent me to proclaim freedom for the prisoners and recovery of sight to the blind, to release the oppressed and to proclaim the year of the Lord's favor" (Isa. 61:1, 2). The signs and wonders that followed gave evidence that Jesus was the fulfillment of that prophecy, the Holy Spirit-anointed servant of the most High God.

Third, Jesus constantly spoke of the Holy Spirit, teaching His followers that they, like He, would need to walk in an intimate relationship with the Spirit. Jesus taught the disciples that God was graciously willing to give the Holy Spirit to all who would ask (Luke 11:11-13). He said that the Spirit would flow from their inner lives like a stream of living water (John

7:36-39). Jesus encouraged the disciples to believe that the Holy Spirit would help them when they were brought before religious and political authorities (Luke 12:11, 12). He promised that He would send the Holy Spirit to be with them after He returned to heaven. Jesus said that the Holy Spirit would come to teach them, comfort them (John 14:26), and guide them into all truth (John 16:13). He was to become their Counselor (John 14:26). Jesus was teaching them that the ministry of the Holy Spirit enables ordinary Christians to do extraordinary things for God and His kingdom.

Pentecost

On the day that Jesus was to ascend to heaven, He gathered His disciples to give them final instructions. He reaffirmed His commission to them with these words: "All authority in heaven and earth has been given to me. Therefore go and make disciples, baptizing them in the name of the Father,

---

The ministry of the Holy Spirit enables ordinary Christians to do extraordinary things for God and His kingdom.

Son, and Holy Spirit, and teaching them to obey everything that I have commanded you. And surely I am with you always, to the very end of the age" (Matt. 28:18-20). Jesus then told them to stay in Jerusalem and wait for the gift of the Holy Spirit. Jesus said that He would not tell them when this would happen, but if they waited as instructed, they would receive power from the Holy Spirit that would enable them to change the world (Acts 1:4-8).

The disciples did wait, and they prayed. They gathered together in an upper room for fifty straight days. And then it happened. Suddenly a violent wind began to blow through the house where they were meeting. Tongues of fire supernaturally appeared on their heads and they were gloriously filled with the Holy Spirit. They began to speak in other languages as the Spirit enabled them. They had received what Jesus had promised, a supernatural anointing of the Spirit's power and presence. They spilled into the streets with great joy and excitement, and they preached the gospel of Christ. Thousands responded in faith, and the first-century church was born (Acts 2:1-47). The Holy Spirit turned a group of fearful men and women into a kingdom army that would go on to transform the world.

The book of Acts tells about the powerful ministry of the Holy Spirit as He moved through the disciples. Multitudes of people turned to Christ. The disciples were used of God to perform healings and miracles that were astonishing. People were delivered from demonic darkness, angels intervened in human events, and the dead were raised to new life. The followers of Christ walked in incredible power, just as Jesus had promised. These average men and women, who were not always clued in to what Christ was about on earth, became mighty warriors for God. They had gone from spiritual poverty to supernatural power under the anointing of the Holy Spirit. The presence of the Holy Spirit had become the qualifying mark of the Lord's community.

Paul wrote:

> *When I came to you, bothers, I did not come with eloquence or superior wisdom as I proclaimed to you the testimony about God. For I resolved to know nothing while I was with you except Jesus Christ and him crucified. I came to you in weakness and fear, and with*

much trembling. My message and my preaching were
not with wise and persuasive words, but with a demon-
stration of power, so that your faith might not rest on
men's wisdom, but on God's power. (I Cor. 2:1-4)

Paul is clearly saying that demonstrations of the Holy Spirit's power were the greatest apology for the Christian faith in the first century. Words and wisdom were simply not enough. Those that preached Christ and the cross verified the truth of their claims through the supernatural ministry of the Holy Spirit. The followers of Christ had been empowered to minister like Christ and it was thrilling.

What Happened?

The Christian experience in many churches and seminaries is often about words. Pastors spend time talking about Christian belief with few if any demonstrations of spiritual power in the local church. It is almost as if the Trinity has become the Father, Son, and Holy Bible. There do not seem to be opportunities for people to really experience the person of the Holy Spirit.

Christian have become so conditioned to a powerless Christianity that they do not even question the Spirit's absence. They have grown accustomed to a knowledge-based faith without power. Healings, miracles, and deliverances are to be read about, not experienced. Some groups have even explained away the supernatural component of Christianity, saying that it all ended with the first century, even though much of church history indicates otherwise. The result of this is tragic and has caused many to view the church as uninteresting and irrelevant.

I have often wondered what Paul would think if he visited one of our twenty-first century church services. He would probably want to know who it was that tamed the church. In the first century, meeting in Jesus' name was so dynamic that you had to think twice about going. People were known to drop dead from the power of His presence. Today, in many places, death in church is boredom induced.

Churches today have fallen into the very habits that His word warned about. They have become ignorant of spiritual things (I Cor. 12:1). Our Enlightenment thinking has prioritized reason above the supernatural, and educational narrow-

---

People do not have the Spirit because they do not ask for His presence to be manifest in their lives.

---

ness has infiltrated the church. Many Christians have also tried to limit the Holy Spirit (I Thess. 5:19), and put out His fire. Their own discomfort and desire to control has driven them to quench His work. And for many there is a serious sin problem that grieves the Spirit and restricts His activity (Eph. 4:30). Relational turmoil in the local church stifles the free flow of the Holy Spirit's power.

But the worst problem is lack of faith. People do not have the Spirit because they do not ask for His presence to be manifest in their lives (Luke 11:9-13), failing to believe that faith alone is the key (Gal. 3:5). Many believers have become used to working in their own power and ability, as though Christianity were a journey taken in their own strength. This attitude is exhausting at best and, at worst, ineffective. Countless churches are burdened in powerless Christianity and it does not need to be that way, for God still invites His people to receive power from on high.

Be Filled with The Spirit

Paul commanded Christians to be filled with the Holy Spirit (Eph. 5:18). His words are not an invitation, but an imperative spoken to all who follow the way of Jesus. For Paul, being born again in the Spirit is the beginning of the Christian life. But, as with Jesus, there comes a time when the anointing of the Spirit's presence fills the servants of the Lord. A more literal translation of this text would read, "Keep on being filled with the Spirit." Christians have the opportunity to daily seek His empowerment for life and ministry. It is available to believers as a present reality, over and over again.

This experience is not one that the believer can initiate. It is a work done by the Spirit of God upon those who wait in faith. And it is not reserved for spiritual superstars. Paul's command was given in the plural, which means that it is for every believer. And, quite importantly, the filling of the Holy Spirit has a real, experiential component. People who walk in His power feel His presence with them. The intensity certainly varies, but His power is a tangible reality.

The Holy Spirit will move believers into a naturally supernatural dimension of Christian service. The twenty-first century church will then move forward as it did in the first century. It will advance with demonstrations of God's power. The lost will be found, the hateful turned to lovers, the enslaved set free, and the wounded healed. This is the work of the kingdom and the greatest testimony to the reality of Jesus Christ.

Facing A Crossroads

Many Christian leaders would be put off with the notion that the Holy Spirit wants to move through people in a supernatural way. They stand at this crossroad and warn of excess and emotionalism, urging believers to opt for disuse rather than potential misuse. They talk of prioritizing the Word above experience, and yet discount what the Bible teaches about the ministry of signs and wonders. They go beyond preaching faith before feeling, to a dull faith with little feeling. These people are like clouds without water, and the thirsty find no satisfaction from their message. People want to find the promised living water and will follow those who have found it. The path of least resistance in this case leads to a head full of facts, but a heart void of God's experiential presence.

The way has been mapped out for Christians by Jesus Christ. He walked in the power of the Holy Spirit and still commands His followers to do the same today. The Promised Gift is still available, given abundantly to all who will ask. His disciples waited upon that gift and were transformed into kingdom warriors to be reckoned with. There is absolutely no good reason for the people of Christ to walk in spiritual poverty when the Holy Spirit is offering to anoint Christians with His presence. The path is clear before believers: a dynamic journey of supernatural dimensions that ushers in kingdom realities into day-to-day life.

For people who are longing to take this path but still hesitant, I offer these suggestions. First, prayerfully go to God's word and read about the ministry of Jesus. The Gospels include important teaching about the Holy Spirit, and the book of Acts is full of His presence. Paul also has written a great deal in his letters that is essential to walking in the Spirit's presence and power.

Second, read books about the Holy Spirit and biographies of great Christian leaders who have walked with Him through life. Third, find a place to talk about the Holy Spirit with other interested believers. The very conversation will ignite fire. Fourth, attend gatherings of Christians were the balanced ministry of the Holy Spirit is evident. Prayer meetings and Bible studies could be a great place to start. Finally, pray in faith and ask the lord for the promised gift. Jesus said that the Father would generously give the Spirit to all who ask. Believers should take Him at His word and wait in expectation.

I am deeply grateful for what Jesus has done in my life through the presence of the Holy Spirit. Christian living has moved far beyond rational understanding to an experienced reality. The Holy Spirit has quickened my heart to His presence, and empowered me to participate in the ministry of the kingdom. There is nothing like it. There have been risks, but God's word and people have provided great guardrails for the journey. The Holy Spirit has introduced me to an intimacy I previously had not known, and a power to serve I had not anticipated. It has been a transforming path to take. And in light of some of the conflict that awaits, it is a relationship necessary to survival. Remember the promise, "If you wait, He will come."

9 / Conflict

Many Christians have a serious blind spot when it comes to spiritual warfare. Educated in a western, Enlightenment-informed worldview, they look at life through a prejudiced lens that filters out the supernatural. More than a few believers would relegate the idea of demons and devils to the realm of myth and fantasy, a remnant of what they believe to be a less sophisticated understanding of reality. That is unfortunate, because the battle is real, and countless Christians are assaulted on the journey because they do not know how to address matters of evil supernaturalism.

There are plenty of things that happen in life that "the devil didn't make me do." But the forces of the evil one do work in the shadows to lure people away from God. A fundamental strategy of darkness is to tempt Christians to doubt what God has said to be true, enticing believers to choose a less costly path for life. If Christians wonder if what I am writing is true, they need to consider the life of Jesus, who experienced this warfare firsthand.

Following His incredible encounter with God at the Jordan River, Jesus was led by the Holy Spirit into the desert.

The Old Testament calls this place Jeshimmon, a place of devastation that is marked by dust heaps, crumbling limestone, jagged rocks, and heat that resembles a blast furnace. Jesus did not go to the wilderness for a short break before starting His public ministry. He was there for a long season of testing, as the devil worked to lure Him away from God's mission. Eugene Peterson has captured this story well in his paraphrase of scripture, *The Message*:

> *Now Jesus, full of the Holy Spirit, left the Jordan and was led by the Spirit into the wild. For forty wilderness days and nights he was tested by the Devil. He ate nothing during those days, and when the time was up he was hungry.*
>
> *The devil, playing on his hunger, gave the first test: "Since you're God's Son, command this stone to turn into a loaf of bread."*
>
> *Jesus answered by quoting Deuteronomy: "It takes more than bread to really live."*
>
> *For the second test he led him up and spread out all the kingdoms of the earth on display at once. Then the Devil said, "They're yours in all their splendor to serve your pleasure. I'm in charge of them all and can turn them over to whomever I wish. Worship me and they're yours, the whole works."*
>
> *Jesus refused, again backing his refusal with Deuteronomy; "Worship the Lord your God and only the Lord your God. Serve him with absolute single-heartedness."*
>
> *For the third test the Devil took him to Jerusalem and put Him on top of the Temple. He said, "If you are God's Son, jump. It's written, is it not, that 'he has placed you in the care of angels to protect you; they will catch you; you won't so much as stub your toe on a*

stone'?" "Yes," said Jesus, "and it is also written, "don't you dare tempt the Lord your God.""

This completed the testing. The Devil retreated temporarily, lying in wait for another opportunity.

Satan assaulted Christ when he was most vulnerable, tempting him to compromise the call of God upon his life. The evil one tried to get Jesus to question the word He heard from God, that He was His beloved Son. Satan tempted Jesus to use his powers for selfish gain. Satan even attempted to appeal to greed, promising Jesus power and wealth if only He would turn away from God's appointed path. Jesus stood

---

Any serious Christian who has followed Jesus on the journey knows the reality of spiritual warfare.

---

firm in the trial, using the Word of God as His defense against the lies of the evil one. The devil left, but as scripture teaches, he was lying in wait all the while for another opportunity to attack the Lord.

Jesus was engaged in spiritual warfare throughout his life on earth. He regularly confronted the powers of darkness by casting demons out of those in bondage (Luke 8:26-39; 9:37-45; 11:14-26). Satan even tried to use those closest to Christ to lead Him astray, speaking words through them that would draw Jesus away from God's plan (Matt. 16:21-38). In the end, Satan was able to influence Judas to betray Jesus and send Him to the cross (Luke 22:3). Satan hated Christ and wanted Him destroyed. But the cross was not a defeat for Jesus, it was His greatest victory. He not only paid for sin on

Calvary, He defeated the forces of evil and turned the curse of crucifixion into the greatest blessing humankind has ever known (Col. 2:13-15).

The victory belongs to Christ, but the battle rages on until the final day when Satan will be destroyed eternally. Those who follow Christ will face the power of the tempter, just as the Lord did. Jesus knew this and prayed to the Heavenly Father that they would be protected from the evil one after He returned to heaven (John 17:15). Any serious Christian who has followed Jesus on the journey knows the reality of spiritual warfare.

Walking in His Strength

Exactly how are Christians to combat the evil one? What weapons and strategies are available to keep believers from being easy prey along the path? These critical questions have been answered by the Apostle Paul in one of the best teachings on spiritual warfare available to God's people. It comes in his letter to the Ephesian church, chapter six. Paul's first admonition is that all who follow Christ must "be strong in the Lord and in the strength of His might" (Eph. 6:10). This is not simply to be an intellectual assent to the fact that God is strong and mighty. Paul is encouraging Christians to be experientially empowered by God. God's people must be in partnership with the Holy Spirit and able to walk in the power that only He can provide.

Why is this so critical to moving forward successfully with Jesus? Paul wrote that many of the most severe battles people face on the way will not come from flesh and blood. They will come from the powers of darkness at work in the spiritual realm that is all around us. Paul had experienced the savage nature of spiritual warfare and wrote this chapter as a way of equipping believers to stand firm when trials come.

He took this conflict seriously, particularly when he

chose to use the Greek word, *pale*, in verse twelve, which is commonly translated *struggle*. This word could equally be translated *wrestle*. The term was often used in reference to a wrestling match where the loser was blinded for life as punishment for being defeated. This was probably a metaphorical reference to what Paul saw as the design of the dark forces. Satan wants to blind Christians to the reality of God's kingdom and will work to do whatever is necessary to bring them into that darkness. It is critical that Christians walk in the strength and might of the Lord.

Paul went on to encourage Christians to daily put on the armor of God. He uses this metaphor to emphasize that there will be battles and Christians need to be thoroughly equipped to defeat the evil one. The armor is only good if it is worn, and Paul suggests that it be a constant part of the covering Christians wear. Paul uses the image to help believers see how important it is that they daily remember and claim the help and promises of the Lord. Practically, Christians should embrace these truths in prayer constantly, as a way of standing against the temptations of the evil one.

The belt of truth is to be worn around the waist (Eph. 6:14). This belt secures believers against the deception that Satan uses to get believers to doubt what God has declared to be true. Believers must daily declare the promises of God and the truth of ultimate victory in Christ, no matter how bad the battle seems at the time. Jesus is alive, He did rise from the dead, and He does sit at the right hand of God in heaven. This is the truth and Christians must be ready at all times to run into battle boldly declaring that Jesus is Lord.

Christians also wear the breastplate of righteousness (Eph. 6:14). The evil one will try to deal fatal blows to believers by accusing them of past sin. He will endeavor to make them feel guilty about past failures, to convince them that they are unworthy losers who have no business following

Jesus Christ. To combat this Christians are to wear the nature of Christ as their covering and move forward confidently to claim all that is theirs is Jesus. They are to declare daily that they are new creations in Christ and given the inheritance of all saints in Jesus.

Paul instructs believers to put on the shoes of peace. Earlier in Ephesians Paul wrote that through the blood of Christ all Christians have been brought near to God. He has established a relationship with them that will last for all eternity (Eph. 2:12-13). Peace with the Lord is what the journey is all about. The Father sent Jesus in order to draw all who believe into His loving embrace. Every step of the way believers will find that God is shaping them for deeper intimacy with Him, which brings a peace that surpasses understanding. The evil one will try to convince believers otherwise, but with the shoes of the gospel in place, Christians can move on with the Lord to greater levels of relationship, security, and joy.

The helmet of salvation is another vital part of the armor (Eph. 6:17). It protects the mind against all the lies of the evil

---

Spiritual warriors know that prayer can open the heavens and summon the angelic host to help in the day of evil.

---

one. Roman soldiers always had symbols of previous victories placed upon their battle helmets. These served as reminders of great victories in the past, and assured them of future victories. That metaphor works perfectly when discussing spiritual warfare. The evil one will move forward with great threat, trying to convince believers that sure defeat is at hand. But the helmet of salvation signifies that Jesus is the Overcoming One, and that He will once again enable Christians to march ahead with Him in victory.

The evil one is the deceiver who uses lies to tempt Christians to abandon their walk with Christ. He constantly shoots at believers with arrows of doubt, harassment, and oppression, trying to get them to turn and run in fear. But faith will serve as a shield against these tactics, extinguishing the power of his words, as Christians trust in the power and promise of Christ (Eph. 6:16). Faith is a gift of God and wise followers are always asking for more.

Finally, Christians wield the sword of the Spirit, which is the word of God (Eph. 6:17). The evil one will tempt people by appealing to the hungers, desires, and struggles with pride. He tried this strategy with Jesus and he will attempt the same with all of Jesus' followers. And so, just like Jesus, Christians should use God's word as a sword. When the battle gets close and the temptation strong, Christians should call for the Holy Spirit to bring God's Word to mind, and face down the evil one with the words, "it is written."

Paul's final words about spiritual warfare have to do with prayer and discernment, two vital weapons in the Christian arsenal (Eph. 6:18). He instructed Christians to be ready to pray all kinds of prayer at a moment's notice. Spiritual warriors know that there is power behind prayer. It can open the heavens and summon the angelic host to help in the day of evil. Prayer is a serious discipline for Christians and not for the faint of heart. It helps believers touch the spiritual realm where the true battle for hearts is waged. Prayer is the door to supernatural power and divine intervention, and should be a familiar place of entry for serious believers.

Discernment is a discipline of watchfulness, used by Christians to see the enemy coming long before he gets close enough to do harm. Discernment involves knowing the kind

of terrain where evil lurks, the places in the path where he
is likely to strike, and the deceptions he uses along the journey. Discernment helps Christians pay attention to commonly used battle strategies and helps them prepare for any and
all assaults. Paul said that Christians should be alert, just like
a soldier on watch in a war zone. Any soldier who has
walked sentry knows that watchfulness can be a matter of life
or death. This world is occupied territory and wise Christians
are aware of that every hour of every day. They must move
along the path with eyes open, well armed, and strong in the
power of God. Spiritual warfare is not a game; it is a real battle and Christians are the number one target.

Facing A Crossroads

Christians are constantly called to choose. As they journey through life with Christ, they will repeatedly stand at
crossroads facing decisions about which way to go. And
sooner or later the fork in the road will involve the matter of
spiritual warfare. One path set before believers will be the
way of least resistance: a Christianity defined by thinkers
who have little or no room for such notions as evil spirits.
The spiritual realm is, for them, mostly a myth relegated to a
more primitive, non-scientific time.

I once studied a theologian in seminary who said that no
thinking Christian, living in a day of electricity and automo-
biles, could take the notion of angels and evil spirits seriously. His arguments were filled with ridicule toward those who
thought otherwise, and many over the years agreed with his
conclusions, if not in theory, at least in practice. For some,
this is an appealing way to go. But is definitely not the path
of Jesus. And by not considering Satan's presence, believers
become easy targets for painful and devastating attacks.
Many are wounded, and some are even lost.

Jesus Christ experienced the reality of the spiritual battle, taking on the evil one first hand. He spoke of this regularly with His followers and gave them power and authority to walk as overcomers through life. To follow Jesus on the journey will mean that Christians today must choose to approach life as He did. Anything less is a compromise that plays directly into the hand of Satan.

Christians who want to journey with Jesus Christ must see the reality of spiritual warfare and be daily prepared for battle. There will be conflict. Those who recognize this fact will grow in strength and might. They will be armed to push back the darkness when it presses in to tempt them away from Christ. And in time they will serve Jesus as warriors, sent to rescue people who are prisoners of the evil one.

10 / Communication

Mark includes in his gospel a very instructive story about the priorities of Jesus. Soon after beginning His ministry, the Lord visited the home of Peter and Andrew. It turned out that Peter's mother-in-law was sick with a fever, and they told the Lord that she was not feeling well. Jesus went in, took her by the hand, and helped her to her feet. The fever immediately left and she began to wait on all her visitors. When the news of this healing spread around Capernaum, people began to bring the sick and demon possessed to Simon and Andrew's home. The Bible says that the whole town gathered outside the door as Jesus healed various diseases and drove out demons from people (Mark 1:29-31).

What a great opportunity! All the Lord would have needed to do was let the news spread into the neighboring towns. People would have rushed to His side for healing and they would have believed that He was the Son of God. His healing power would have been the key to fulfilling His mission. But that is precisely what the Lord did not do!

While everyone was sleeping that night, Jesus went off to be alone. He wanted to spend time with His Father in prayer.

When Simon and Andrew arose and saw that Jesus was gone they went looking for Him. When they finally found Him they could hardly wait to tell Jesus that everyone back in the town was looking for Him. There were sick people everywhere, and many others standing around to watch the miracles. What could have been better? It was instant success. He had gone from unknown evangelist to local celebrity in the blink of an eye. It seemed as if the hand of God's blessing was all over them.

But what did Jesus do? He told His followers to leave, to move on to the nearby villages because He wanted to preach. He said that preaching was the reason He came, and even something as powerful as a healing ministry was not going to keep Him from fulfilling that calling. Any hardworking preacher would say that this decision took a great deal of strength. It is not easy to gather a crowd of people to hear someone preach. I know, because I spent many years doing it, and there were few times that people rushed the door to hear what I had to say. But healing—that is a different matter.

Sick people will pack any size hall if genuine healing is happening there. If a speaker was gifted to heal, he would have an open door to incredible opportunity, at least as I might evaluate it. But Jesus was not so given to compromising priorities. He came to preach the gospel of the Kingdom of God, and not even large crowds and apparent success would keep Him from God's plan.

Jesus arrived on earth with a message from God. He went from village to village telling people that the Kingdom of God was infiltrating this enemy occupied planet, and God was going to set them free. He proclaimed that God was offering forgiveness to all who had entered the rebellion, and promised them eternal life if they believed in what Jesus came to do. Jesus told people that God loved them lavishly, and sent His Son to save them. He assured people that He did not come to point out all their mistakes and condemn them, but to give them everlasting life. All they needed to do was receive and believe (John 3:14-21). Jesus would take care of the rest.

No wonder that Jesus' message was called good news. Indeed, it was so good it was sometimes hard for people to really believe. Many said that his message did not come from God. Why would God just hand out so great a promise with-

---

Jesus went from village to village telling people that the Kingdom of God was infiltrating this enemy-occupied planet.

---

out cost to them? But this salvation could not be earned; it was not the reward for good behavior or the result of good deeds. It was a gift. Many of the most poor, needy, and outcast people of that day chose to believe because the sermons Christ preached brought hope. And everywhere Jesus went, He preached this word.

Bringing Good News
At the end of His ministry, following the resurrection, Jesus told His followers to keep preaching the good news of God's love. He commissioned His followers to spread that word to every person, of every people group, in every nation on the face of the earth (Matt. 28:18-20; Mark 16:15-18). Jesus said that when people believed the good news they would be saved and should be baptized. And He warned them that if people did not believe the message, they would be condemned for all

eternity (Mark 16:16). The message held the promise of life and death, and the responsibility to communicate that good news now lay in the hands of the disciples.

The followers of Christ did exactly what Jesus said. Following Pentecost they preached about Jesus and salvation everywhere. At first they ministered in Jerusalem and the surrounding region, and thousands believed. Within a few short years they moved out into regions beyond, particularly under the ministry of the Apostle Paul. What began with a handful of followers after the crucifixion grew within a few decades to tens of thousand of believers in places as far away as Rome. Love for Christ, the presence of the Spirit, and a heart for the lost moved them forward, even when the end of the road brought martyrdom. They were under orders and determined that nothing would keep them from sharing the message of God's love, made available to all through Jesus Christ.

Where Are We Now?

In 1982 I had the opportunity to study with the British Christian scholar, David Watson. The experience still stands as a highlight of all my academic work. In one lecture Watson shared the following insight about evangelism. He said that, based on the ratio between the number of Christians there are today and the number of people accepting Christ per year, it takes one thousand Christians three hundred and sixty-five days to win one person to Christ. I had to sit and think about that. It seemed too hard to believe. Many people choose to follow Christ, but few of them turn to share the gospel with others. As a result, many people are not having the opportunity to meet Christ and follow Him in life. This is not only true in this country, but is a fact all around the world.

I often wonder why Christ left the responsibility of communicating the good news to people. Surely He knew that there was a real potential that the job would not be done.

Regardless, the hope of many rests with the willingness of the few. In his letter to the Roman Christians, Paul wrote compellingly about this great need:

> *Everyone who calls on the name of the Lord will be saved. How then will they call on the one they have not believed in? And how can they believe in the one of whom they have not heard? And how can they hear without someone preaching to them? And how can they preach unless they are sent? 'How beautiful are the feet of those who bring good news'...Faith comes by hearing the message, and the message is heard through the word of Christ.* (Rom. 10:13-15,17).

Lost and broken people need to hear the message of salvation and Christians are to do the communicating. This does not simply mean professional preachers and missionaries who travel to other towns and nations to spread the good news. It involves all Christians, regularly sharing the good news with family members, neighbors, co-workers and employers. All Christians are called to communicate the message of Christ, to witness to the greatness of God's saving love. This is Christ's commission to His church.

There are several reasons why this is not happening with all Christians. First, many have not allowed God to break their hearts for a lost and dying world. It is easy to have tunnel vision in this world, and limit one's concerns to his or her own selfish needs. But there are millions of people who need to hear and receive the wonderful news of life in Jesus Christ. God is passionate about them and wants to set them free. These dear people are living enslaved by sin and will spend eternity in darkness unless they believe the good news of Christ. Christians need to feel the heartbeat of the Father who longs to bring lost people home. If Christians ask, God will give them that heart.

Second, some Christians have not been told that this is their responsibility. Many believers do not search God's word for themselves, relying instead on pastors and teachers to feed them. But not all pastors prioritize the message of salvation or call people to become involved in Christian witness. Good works may be emphasized, but the notion of communicating the gospel is not taught. This is tragic, because the message of the Kingdom was the number one priority of Jesus Christ and His disciples. Five times the gospels command believers to spread that good news. It is an important word for the church.

> ## *The message of the Kingdom was the number one priority of Jesus Christ and His disciples.*

Third, many Christians do not want to share the good news because they are put off by the confrontational evangelistic methods they have seen modeled by other believers. And frankly, there are right. Few people ever respond to the gospel because someone leaves a tract at the restaurant or hands it to a passerby on the street. Such methods feel manipulative and confrontational to many Christians so they bow out. The best means of sharing the faith are relational. There is no better way to attract a person to Christ than by becoming a true friend to them. Sharing common interests builds deep bonds between people. Genuine caring is always the best bridge for Christ to cross between two people. Opportunities to talk about the good news will arise naturally, and broken people will have an honest chance to respond to the gift of life in Christ.

Fourth, many Christians have the idea that people will be put off with them if they share their faith. Images of angry reactions and intense confrontations abound, and it becomes much easier to believe that being a Christian is a private matter between a person and God. My experience could not be further from this. I have found that men and woman are thirsty for living water. They want life to have meaning and the issue of death looms in their minds daily. When I have had the opportunity to talk about Jesus and what He has done in my life, the vast majority of people have been willing to listen. This is particularly true when I have taken the time to get to know them and demonstrate genuine caring. People are put off with hard sell and empty promises. But the genuine article is always difficult to dismiss. Thirsty people still want water.

Finally, many Christians hesitate to share the good news because they are not confident that they can tell it accurately. That fear is understandable, so it is important for churches to help people learn the basic themes of the Christian message. In truth, most people who are lost do not need chapter and verse. They want to see the gospel lived out in another person's life in a way that is attractive. More than a few believers have told me that friends actually brought up the subject of Christ to them because they saw there was something different about their lives. That is the way it should be.

Christians can be very effective talking to others by sharing a simple testimony that identifies four things: what life was like before they came to Christ, how they came to know they needed Christ, what they did to accept Christ, and how life has changed since they received Christ. Countless people have been transformed by hearing the gospel shared in this very way. As believers move forward as communicators, they can interweave key scriptures into their testimony, like John 3:16. More people have come to Christ through that verse than any other passage in all of scripture. It is the entire gospel in one sentence.

Facing A Crossroads

I often think about what my life would have been like had I not heard the gospel of Christ and believed. It would have been a journey of sadness that led to great pain and ultimate destruction. I am so thankful to the people who turned on the path and invited me to follow them in following Jesus. It has been the most transformational choice I have ever made. The invitation to accept Christ opened the way for me to experience the presence of God, and that has become the treasure of my life. I have experienced the truth of Jesus' statement that He is the way, and the truth, and the life (John 14:6). By His grace I have been brought near to the Father and touched by the power of salvation. All of this, and more, happened because someone was willing to communicate.

I have heard Christians talk about another path. There, people believe that a person can find God apart from Christ. They say that there are many ways to God, and Jesus is only one of them. Some who take that path even argue that it is religious bigotry to suggest that a person needs Jesus, that He is the only way. To them, all roads lead to heaven, and there is no real need to share the good new of Christ Jesus. This is without question the way of least resistance, and it leads to a confusing and dark nowhere land.

Christians are called to take the path of Jesus Christ. He preached the good news, became the good news, and commissioned his followers to communicate the good news everyday, everywhere. Jesus longs to bring the broken and lost along on the journey, and wants His followers to share that gospel with them. He died so that they, like all believers, could grow in intimacy with God, experience conformity to Christ, be secure in their identity as God's children, and mature into healing servants.

Jesus has a heart for the whole world, and has asked believers to tell one and all about the Gift of Life. So much depends upon Christians joining Christ at this crossroads. The day will come when all will face this fork in the road. Will we go the way of Jesus and tell of good news? The whole world is depending on it.

11 / Communion

J esus knew how to care for Himself and refill His spiritual reserves. No matter how busy He was, how great the need, or how large the crowds, Jesus would regularly get away and commune with God. He saw His life as intricately linked to God and continually came apart to be with Him. Jesus told His followers that He was sent by the Father (John 20:21), to do the will of the Father (John 6:40), and teach the truth that the Father would give Him (John 7:16). He said that He was dependent upon the Father for His ministry (John 6:44), and would only do what He saw the Father doing (John 5:19). Jesus made it clear that He was determined to glorify the Father with His life (John 17:1), and ultimately return to the Father in heaven (John 20:17). Jesus loved His Father and regularly stepped out of the busy pace of life to be with Him.

Many important events took place with Jesus while He was with God in prayer or directly following such times. This was true of Jesus' wilderness temptation and with His trans-figuration. Jesus refocused His primary ministry from healing to preaching in response to a night in prayer, and chose His disciples immediately after being alone with the Father in prayer. Immediately before Jesus walked on water He had sent His disciples away so that He could spend time on the mountainside communing with God. And the night before the crucifixion, Jesus hid away in prayer, desperately needing the strength and comfort that only the Father could provide.

The disciples were well aware that the authority of Christ's ministry was directly related to the time He spent in communing prayer. Of all the things they could have asked Jesus to teach them, prayer was the priority for them (Luke 11:1-13). They had been with Jesus when He went to a private place to meet with God and knew that Jesus received power from those times. When Jesus ascended to heaven He told the dis-

---

The authority of Christ's ministry was directly related to the time He spent in communing prayer.

---

ciples to wait in Jerusalem for the Promise. They did as He said, and spent the time in constant prayer (Acts 1:14).

The Holy Spirit did come and from that moment onward the followers of Christ walked in power and prioritized prayer. They received visions in prayer, experienced healings from prayer, were rescued by prayer, and sought direction in prayer. In many ways communing with God in prayer became their preoccupation. It was a channel of intimacy and power for them. It is no wonder then why Paul instructed Christians to be continually in prayer (I Thess. 5: 17). He believed that communing with the Father in prayer would bring a degree of peace and protection that was beyond understanding (Phil. 4:7). For first-century Christians, to follow

Christ was to be a person of prayer. It was the way of Jesus and had become the passion of those who intended to walk as He did through life.

A Hard Lesson to Learn

Most Christians know deep within that they should be spending time communing with the Lord. In fact, many believers I talk with experience some level of guilt about not meeting with God. They feel bad because it just isn't happening in their lives. A lot of sincere Christians make well-intentioned resolutions about devotional disciplines that soon fade away from lack of effectiveness. Eventually, many believers just give up on it all, convinced that intimate communion is a gift reserved exclusively for super-saints. This is as true for professional Christian workers as it is for laypeople. I have had innumerable conversations with pastors, counselors and missionaries who have essentially given up on the idea of a dynamic prayer life. What results is a spiritual bankruptcy that is soon noticeable to all. A prayerless life is a powerless life.

Several identifiable obstacles keep people from times of personal communion. First among these is the busyness of our culture. Christians have been deeply affected by the ethos of the American dream. From the earliest days of life people are conditioned to achieve and acquire. They are prepared for performance and praised for how far they get ahead in life. To do this, people are taught to work hard and spend long hours reaching for the brass ring. In many families both parents work which necessitates finding surrogates to help raise their children. People have traded away the opportunity for personal depth for material breadth. The resulting spiritual poverty is epidemic.

Christians are not free from the drive to stay busy. They are not only trying to balance job and family requirements, but also have pressure to be active in the local church. This activity is usually service oriented, giving people yet another thing to do in their already hectic schedule. In my observation most pastors are workaholics caught in a destructive pattern of trying to accomplish kingdom work in their own strength. The churches they serve do not help, because they seldom encourage their leaders to get apart with God. They are evaluated by the number of meetings they attend and visits they make, rather than the sense of empowerment they have from communing with the Lord. People-pleasing and performance have become addictions that drive God's people to stay engaged twenty-four hours a day, seven days a week. Many Christians respond to the call to prayer with the words, "Where will I find the time?" Emergency living has replaced the urgent personal need for time apart.

Second, many Christians have difficulty being alone and silent. I notice that people often need to have people and noise around them to feel safe and secure. One friend told me recently that when he finally got alone and quiet he was unbelievably anxious. He said that he had to leave his place of solitude because the silence was deafening to him. He told me that he felt worse after trying to meet with God than he did before. "So why bother?" The truth is that the anxiety was always shouting within him, but he was using people and activity to silence it. When he finally slowed down enough to listen, the internal voice of upheaval frightened him. He thought that the problem came with the silence. He was wrong. The silence revealed what all of his activity was masking. He needed to press through the pain and allow God to meet Him at the point of deep need. He needed a healing touch that could only come through intimate communion with the Lord.

Third, most Christians do not know what to do during the time apart with the Lord. I have more than once heard someone say that they tried to set a day apart with the Lord, but found it boring. I am sure first-century Christians would have been bewildered by that response, but for many believers today it is an honest evaluation of their experience. In part this happens because people are so results driven that if something isn't happening within the first few minutes, they write the experience off as ineffective. But for other Christians being apart with God meant trying to dutifully make their way through a devotional checklist of activities. They believed they had to do certain "things" as part of a daily quiet time, for which they would someday be held accountable. And so they "do" devotions, all the while never meeting the One who is to be the focus of the time apart. People do not experience this for long before they grow frustrated with the concept. After a while, the obstacles to communing with the Lord seem insurmountable and people just give up, quietly carrying the guilt and living through the deep emptiness.

Positioning for his Presence

Christians have been made to experience intimate fellowship with the Lord. Granted, it will not be easy, particularly in our world. But believers can, with the help of the Holy Spirit, grow to commune regularly with God. It is unquestionably a critical part of the journey, and Jesus has walked the path ahead of us to make a way. Several practical suggestions can help in renewing people's experience of coming apart with God. But we must remember that the world around us, the unseen enemy, and our own weaknesses will keep this from being an easy commitment to fulfill. But when they do, it will not be long before communion is the first place we want to go and the place where we stay the longest in the Christian life.

First, believers who are struggling to commune with God must clarify the purpose of such time. It is not a duty to be performed. Being alone is about making space in life to experience God intimately. It is setting aside the noise of the world in order to hear the whispers of a loving Father who wants to spend time with His children. This relationship cannot be forced. It needs to be developed, just as it is with any personal relationship. If Christians approach this time as though they were fulfilling a job or accomplishing something on their spiritual checklist, they will not experience His presence. God will not be pressured into meeting with people because they have worked hard to make something happen. He is not into people-pleasing or impressed by performance. But if Christians sit and wait before the Lord in longing love, two hearts will eventually meet, and the experience will be transformational.

Second, Christians would do well to be honest with the Lord about their own hearts. I have faced this in my own prayer life. After years of struggle I finally came to the place of telling God that I knew my prayer life was empty and that I was not sure I wanted to do anything about it. But, knowing that communing with the Lord was so vital to my life, I asked for help. I prayed that the Holy Spirit would ignite a desire within me to regularly come apart with God. And I also requested that He lead me into an experience of prayer that was real and powerful. With that request, I agreed to begin spending time alone everyday, positioning myself for the Lord's transforming touch. It took time to break through for me, but slowly a new passion and power began to grow. I also began to experience an increased sense of His intimate love and a new effectiveness in ministry. God honored the prayer of honesty and broke in to draw me closer to His embrace.

Third, communing with God also takes time. Christians need to look at this in two important ways. To grow in the Lord believers need to regularly set apart time, over seasons of time. Setting apart time involves daily making space in the schedule for quiet before the Lord. I am not comfortable suggesting how long this needs to be, but certainly it needs to be enough time to silence the noise of the world in order to hear God's voice. Growing in communion with the Lord is much like developing any relationship. It takes an investment. It involves times of honest and deep communication to build intimacy. It also involves developing habits over time. Coming apart cannot be a short-term commitment. It must become a life pattern, not an occasional emphasis. Intimacy and empowerment build as Christians move forward with the Lord over the many changing seasons of life.

Fourth, we need to find a special place. Jesus loved the mountainsides and went there regularly to commune with the Lord. He seemed to particularly enjoy meeting the Father on the Mount of Olives in the Garden of Gethsemane. These loca-

> *Intimacy and empowerment build as Christians move forward with the Lord over the many changing seasons of life.*

tions had become sacred space for Christ, places that drew Him into the Father's presence. Most Christians will find that identifying sacred spaces will help them commune with the Lord. I personally find it helpful if the environment is quiet, comfortable, and conducive to personal reflection. When indoors, I want my sacred space to have pictures, candles, and music available to bring my attention away from the world and upward toward God. If I am outside, I want sacred space to be picturesque, hidden, and inspiring to my spirit. I find that when I regularly meet God in these places, the very thought of going there again places me immediately into His presence. That is part of the benefit of special places. We can even come to them in our mind and have a time of deep fellowship with the Lord even when we are far away from the sacred space.

Finally, spiritual disciplines help us experience deepening levels of communion with the Lord. Spiritual disciplines are activities that for centuries positioned people in God's presence. They must never be seen as tasks that a Christian must do in order to grow. They are channels of grace that position us to meet the Lord. The activity does not force God's hand, but instead invites His presence. There are many disciplines, such as fasting, Bible reading, worship, confession, solitude, silence, and of course prayer. These disciplines can be practiced alone and as part of life in the community of Christ. People should use a variety of disciplines as needed and as the Holy Spirit directs, for each activity helps them catch the wind of God's presence that will take them to increasing levels of intimacy and power.

All believers can practice prayer at three levels. First, they can come before God and list all their concerns and needs. He cares about His children and welcomes their requests. Second, believers should move on to listen for His voice in prayer. God will speak to His children and direct them through life according to His plan. Recognizing His voice may take time, but with the Spirit's help, believers can grow to converse spiritually with the Lord. Third, Christians should simply sit and enjoy His presence. In these times very little will be said, but volumes will be communicated across deep lines of love and devotion.

Facing a Crossroads

What should Christians expect to face when following Jesus Christ? There will be many choices, and one will certainly involve the matter of intimate prayer. The time will come when believers will stand at a crossroads that leads to two very different experiences with God. One, the way of least resistance, will be duty driven and full of busy activity. Christians will be pressured to stay engaged at all times, striving with every ounce of energy to do the work of ministry. But this path leads to increasing levels of emptiness and ineffectiveness. The soul is not filled and the spirit grows weak. Eventually spiritual bankruptcy results.

But Christians who stand at this crossroads will see another way, and Jesus is waiting there. He is calling His followers to come apart and learn about intimate prayer. Jesus recognizes that it will not be easy, that there are obstacles. He knows that many have already struggled to get there in their own strength, and failed. But Jesus still comes, encouraging all to come that way. He promises to help, for Jesus knows that communing prayer is the key to life along the journey, to the ministry that God has given to His own. Jesus invites every believer to experience the transforming power of time spent communing with the Lord. He invites believers to choose. And this very moment is not too soon to begin spending time with Him.

.

12 / Compassion

Most middle and upper class Christians are not in touch with the breadth of human suffering that happens just beyond their view. I am not suggesting that they do not face their own challenges. Like all people, they face the individual trials of sickness and death. I am also not saying that they do not care about such people. I believe their hearts are soft and when they see genuine human need they respond. But there is a degree to which their world has been sanitized, putting pain and suffering out of sight. People with severe mental and physical handicaps are placed in institutions, and only those with friends or family there would have occasion to make any regular contact with them. Middle and upper class Christians know that people who commit crimes are sent to prison, but many are not sure where those institutions might be, and certainly fewer still have ever been inside a lockdown unit. They are relatively unaware of the serious issues facing the criminal justice system.

Middle and upper class Christians have little face-to-face contact with the poor, except when they happen to drive by their neighborhoods on the way to somewhere else. Racial conflict seldom happens in their neighborhoods, though they do read of such events in the newspaper and see news clips on the television. They often offer a prayer when they do see such things, thanking the Lord that they live in a safe community. Such Christians do not battle much with inferior educational systems because the tax base for their districts is generally healthy enough to provide necessary resources. If they are concerned about their children's education in the public school, they often enroll them in private institutions. Homeless people tend to not hang out in the suburbs or farmlands of America. These Christians might care about the issue, but they seldom meet the person.

Broader issues, like the severity of world hunger, illiteracy, the scarcity of medical care, the African AIDS crisis, genocide, and the massive global refugee problem are seldom part of the conversation. Middle and upper class Christians are generally unaware that Sudanese Christians face the constant threat of martyrdom, that there are still tens of thousands of bond slaves in India, and that the oppression of women in some nations is sub-human. Middle and upper class believers do not always understand Christians who fight for social and political justice. Such liberation causes make them uncomfortable. They choose social service over social action, convinced that it is less controversial.

I am not suggesting that these believers do not care. They don't see. They do not have the level of personal contact that causes a broken heart to erupt into loving service. This level of suffering is not in their conscious awareness, and so they attend to what is before them in a much less needy world. I have also found that many Christians do not think about the fact that many of these people are brothers and sisters in Christ. They are blood-bought members of the family who are suffering, and yet few middle and upper class Christians think about that connection. Even if they were not members of the community of Christ, they are people who deserve to receive love and care when life is cruel. Christians are to specialize in that type of ministry, and often do when they truly see what is happening to the broken.

It would be far more honest for me to stop referring to middle and upper class Christians as *they*, and instead say *we*. I am part of that socio-economic group, and know of what I speak. Having grown up as a coal miner's son and having attended a multi-racial school, I thought I was more savvy about such things. But two events changed that for me and showed me a much broader world just beyond my view. In 1985 my wife and children and I moved to New York. I had taken a position at a seminary thirteen miles north of the George Washington Bridge. This brought me into regular contact with New York City, and I fell in love with it. I had many opportunities to minister in the city, in places where crime and poverty were rampant. I came to see that many dear people live under the weight of unimaginable oppression. I could no longer ride through such areas as a sight-seer. I had come to know their names, visit their homes, and see their hearts. I had to get involved at some level.

Jesus came and walked with people in the trials and difficulties of life.

My second epiphany came when I spent a month in a lock-down unit of a psychiatric hospital. Prior to this experience I was thoroughly uneducated about the trials of mental illness. But my eyes were opened. The suffering can be intense and frightening. And the stigma of mental illness is, for many, worn like a scarlet letter for the rest of their lives.

Ignorant people label the person, not the disease, and a degree of ostracizing often occurs.

But from the inside, I found that the people there were absolutely delightful. In fact, they were some of the most interesting and gifted people I have ever met. Today, having personally walked that path, I weep for the emotionally broken and have dedicated much of my life to helping this group of brothers and sisters that was previously unknown to me. I was changed because I became one of them. When Christians walk step by step with people, they grow to learn from them, care for them, and love them more than they would ever dream. But Christians must enter their world to truly feel their pain, just as Jesus did.

Jesus and Compassion

Jesus came and walked with people in the trials and difficulties of life. He was raised in a poor family, and knew what it felt like to live under political oppression. Handicapped and mentally disturbed people were not placed out of sight, but lived on the periphery of the society in full view. Jesus watched the way the broken were treated, forced to call out "unclean" as they passed by, and he knew they were hindered from normal social and religious contact. They were treated as second-class citizens and forced to live without normal human touch and interaction. And this was through no fault of their own, yet they had to bear the weight of the social punishment.

This impacted Jesus deeply, and He was regularly moved with compassion. Granted, the spiritual issues related to redemption were critical to Christ. After all, He gave His life to set people free from the eternal consequences of sin. But Jesus was not untouched by human suffering. He wept at the tomb of Lazarus, fed the hungry from loaves and fishes, gave sight to the blind, cleansed the leper, and set the demonized free. Jesus refused to stone the guilty, ate with tax collectors and sinners, and welcomed a woman with a questionable reputation into his inner circle. And Jesus regularly pulled the masks off of religious leaders who were forcing people to bear heavy ceremonial burdens. He despised the pretense of such games and held little tolerance for those who wanted authority without accountability.

Jesus called all who would follow Him to the same type of action. In the Sermon on the Mount He challenged people to give without expecting anything in return, go the second mile, and share the extra coat with those in need. He said that people should give in secret, and even promised to bless anyone who gave as much as a cup of water in His name (Matt. 5-7). The disciples carried on with this work, and established a ministry to widows and orphans (Acts 6), and distributed help to the poor during a time of great suffering. The Lord's brother, James, hit this issue head on in his letter to the church, when he said that true faith always translates into service to others (James 2:14-29). He warned believers that they must act when they see the poor and hungry, not just bless them with empty words. And the Apostle Paul told Timothy to command Christians to be rich in good deeds and willing to share with all who are in need (I Tim. 6:18). This sacrificial involvement was the way of Christ, and every serious disciple walked that same path.

Down through the centuries of the church, God's people have fought to relieve suffering and oppression wherever they saw it, to the glory of Christ the Lord. Many of the great Christian revivalistic movements also started ministries to the poor and oppressed. William Wilberforce fought against slavery in England, the Wesleys not only preached to save souls, but struck a blow against 18th-century illiteracy. A. B. Simpson went into New York's Hell's Kitchen area and ministered to the forgotten, and General William Booth founded one of the greatest Christian institutions of service the world has ever known, The Salvation Army. Quakers William Penn and John Woolman worked diligently to see that American Indians were treated fairly in colonial America. This represents just a fraction of what the people of Christ have done to relieve the suffering of a broken world. They walked in the footsteps of Christ, and gave far more than a cup of water. Many, including scores of missionaries, gave their very lives in fighting world suffering.

Getting Involved

My daughter Cara, son Aaron, and daughter-in-law Destry spent time overseas before graduating from college. Cara went to the Philippines and Honduras, while Aaron and Destry traveled to Eastern Europe. For each of them, the experience was life changing. I particularly remember the transformation that happened to Aaron following a month in the Ukraine. He had traveled there to work at an orphanage for abandoned children. He was given responsibility to care for a small group of elementary age boys. Every day he helped them get up, dress, go to meals, and prepare for bed. He played with them, held them as they cried, and sat with them in silence when the pain of loneliness was too much to bear.

Aaron learned each of their names and knew about their individual stories. These few boys, unknown to him for twenty-one years, had stolen his heart. Aaron wept as he showed me pictures of them, and spoke from the heart about how precious each boy was. He was delighted with them in every way, and wanted to do all he could to help. They were not statistics to Aaron. They had become people that he loved. He walked into their world and they changed him so much he wanted to help them in return. That is the true nature of incarnational ministry. It is relational, which opens the way to acts of love that set people free.

All Christians can and should be involved in helping those who suffer. And regardless of where believers live, opportunities abound. The very least any Christian can do is pray. I am not, in saying that, minimizing the importance of prayer. It is the doorway to great power. Every believer has access to the Lord through prayer and can make a difference on people's lives. Most church and para-church ministries committed to helping the broken publish prayer letters that list specific needs. Christians can often access those through the internet, through denominational publications, and in the organizations magazines. Christians can easily commit to petitioning the Lord on behalf of those working on the front lines of human need.

Christians can also give money to ministries that care for the broken. There are many responsible organizations serving

---

For Christians to turn a blind eye to a hurting world, they must choose a path other than the one Jesus took.

---

people across the globe. There is hardly a need anywhere in the world where some Christian organization is not trying to help. These ministries are costly, and they welcome gifts from people who want to do their part in touching the world's hurting people. God blesses such giving, because it helps the very people who are the object of His great love and concern. Even a moderate gift can have a great impact on human suffering.

In our society, Christians can stand and be counted. We live in a nation where freedom of speech, freedom of assembly, and the right to vote are protected under the constitution.

This means that people can speak out on issues of unfairness, rally to support the cause of justice, and vote for people who will represent what is righteous and good. Christians in this country are not oppressed, pushed away from the polls, or forbidden to run for political office. For many, these rights are the doorway to great change.

Finally, Christians can and should get involved. Most middle and upper class Christians would find that there is great opportunity to relieve suffering right in their own back yards. The poor are in every community, as well as those who are lonely, handicapped, emotionally oppressed, and overlooked. There are children who need adults who would care to spend time with them, senior citizens who could use a friend, students who could be helped by tutoring, and unemployed men and women who could use help finding a job. There are also many Christian service organizations looking for volunteers for any one of countless programs aimed at helping the less fortunate.

Facing A Crossroads

How can Christians turn a blind eye to a hurting world? To do so they must choose a path other than the one the Jesus took in life. It is the only way. Jesus became human in order to better identify with the human experience. He walked with the broken, listened to their stories, saw them struggle in life, and heard the cry of their tender hearts. This touched Christ deeply, emotionally, and He subsequently reached out to relieve their pain and strengthen them for the journey through life. Jesus did not first require that people follow Him before He would meet their deepest need. He had entirely too much love and integrity for that. He served them because they needed the help. The broken loved Jesus for this. Jesus cared in a way they had never experienced before. And many of them ended up following Him with dedication and joy.

Christians who journey with Jesus will be challenged to help relieve human suffering and need. He does not present this as an option. The path always leads in this direction for Christians. It is an opportunity that the obedient embrace with gratitude and humility. Is there a path of least resistance? Of course, and it leads to a very destructive brand of selfish irrelevance. It is Christian consumerism at its worst, as those with the resources build bigger barns while the hungry die of starvation. It is an irresponsible path that leads to very little that resembles Jesus Christ.

Jesus stands at the crossroads and summons Christians to His side. He commands them to get involved in the needs of people, to learn their names, hear their stories, and fall in love with them as He did. This part of the journey is not all about the Christian, but about how the Christian can take part in changing the world. There is a crossroads, but only one realistic path. There is a decision to be made, but only one viable choice for the Christian to make. It is Jesus, and the call to touch the world in His wonderful name.

13 / Cross

Simon of Cyrene was an innocent bystander who was suddenly thrust into the most important event in human history. Jews from all the surrounding regions around Israel hoped that someday they could make a pilgrimage to celebrate the Passover in Jerusalem. Many times entire families would save up money so that just one of them could be part of that great event. Entire communities would send such blessed travelers off, as if they were all somehow part of that most important journey. The lucky pilgrim likely received a gift of a new cloak or robe to wear during those wonderful days. And it may have been that they would bring back small gifts to everyone who made the trip possible. These special people would return to their communities as celebrities, full of stories about all that they saw and did.

Simon was one of those blessed people who had finally made the journey to Jerusalem. His heart was surely filled with anticipation and hope as he walked the streets, capturing all the sights and sounds of this historic celebration. But he came to a great gathering where people watched as three men were being led to their own crucifixion. Roman soldiers were moving them along with shouts and hostile pushes, taking these men to a slow and painful death. Suddenly, when one of the convicted men fell, the life already draining out from him from a cruel whipping, a soldier looked Simon's way. And before he knew it, the tip of a spear was placed on Simon's shoulder.

Everyone there knew what it meant when the soldier singled out Simon. Though he was dressed to celebrate his trip into the city, Simon was commanded to now make a different journey. He went to the side of the condemned man, Jesus, picked up His cross, and carried it the remainder of the

Jesus knew before the journey ever began that the path would go by Golgotha.

way to Golgotha. Instead of watching this event, he had become a full participant. He could now see the angry stares, hear the shouts from bystanders, and feel the full weight of the cross. His clothes were stained with dirt and Christ's blood as he walked along. In some unexpected way Simon had been drawn close to the side of Jesus, at one and the same time relieving the burden of the cross and helping get to the place of execution.

Simon had come to Jerusalem to remember God's deliverance from the bondage of Egypt centuries before. But he became part of a much greater act of redemption. He thought that this journey would bring him new status in his own small community. But on this day, there was only pain and humiliation. Simon intended simply to watch the events and move on. Instead, he became an important player in the history of the world. The early church father Origen said that on that day Simon carried the cross, not just for Jesus, but for us all. He modeled a very important aspect of Christian living, carrying the cross for the redemption of lost people everywhere.

Many have asked whether Simon of Cyrene ever became a follower of Jesus. There is no way to know for sure. But Mark's gospel mentions that Simon had two sons, Alexander and Rufus. It is almost as if Mark is identifying Simon by referring to his sons, as though members of the church would know them. It is possible. Either way, whether he became a believer or not, Christians everywhere owe Simon of Cyrene a deep debt of gratitude. He carried the cross for Jesus, our Lord. He also demonstrated for us all a very important part of what it means to journey in life with Jesus.

Eyes Set on Jerusalem

Life for Jesus was always cruciform. He knew before the journey ever began that the path would go by Golgotha. Jesus was sent of God to be the final atoning sacrifice for all our sins, and the cross was the place where Jesus paid the price in full (Heb. 10:10). He told His followers that He would suffer and die as part of His mission, and even their vehement protests could not keep Him from this (Matt. 16:21-23). His face was set toward Jerusalem and an appointment with His Father in heaven that would change us all. His blood had to be shed, His body had to be broken, so that people everywhere could be reconciled to God and adopted as His very own children. As Peter wrote in his letter to the church, we Christians were not purchased for God with perishable things like gold and silver. No, the blood of the Lamb was the price of our redemption—from One who was perfect, without spot or blemish (I Pet. 1:18, 19). Jesus, the embodiment of perfect love and tenderness, went to the cross willingly so that believers could be free forever. This is why the cross is not a symbol of shame for Christians, but instead the centerpiece of faith and hope.

Palm Sunday was a day of celebration for the followers of Christ. They had dreaded going into Jerusalem, knowing that the potential for great harm was real and imminent. But as they made their way into the city, a spontaneous parade broke out (Luke 19:28-44). Jesus, riding on a donkey colt, became the fulfillment of prophetic promise. People began to sing praises to God and shout, "Blessed is the king who comes in the name of the Lord!" They threw their cloaks down for the donkey to pass over and waved palm branches in the air in celebration. Granted, when compared to the great parades of power made by Roman legions entering the city, it was a less than impressive affair. But it frightened the religious leaders terribly, setting them on a course that led Jesus straight to Calvary.

The disciples may have gained courage from this display, thinking that momentum was gathering for Jesus to actually take over the throne of Jerusalem. But Jesus knew better. He was destined to go to the cross, and He knew that the climate would change drastically. All the favor would suddenly turn to opposition and songs of praise would soon become shouts of "Crucify him!" Jesus pointed to the sacrificial nature of the cross when He celebrated the last supper with His dearest friends. He told them that the broken bread was His body, given for them. And the wine was blood, poured out as an offering for them (Luke 22:7-38). As Jesus celebrated Passover with them, He knew that very soon he would be the Lamb slain for the sins of all the people.

As all this was happening, the plan had been put into motion for Jesus' arrest. Judas had turned informant, and the religious community had become a tool of the evil one. After spending the final hours of the evening in the Garden of Gethsemane with His disciples, Jesus was taken from them.

He, who had only done good for people, bringing hope and healing to the broken, was abandoned, betrayed, and denied by those closest to Him. After a mockery of a trial, Jesus was stripped, lashed, and led away to a place of crucifixion on the edge of town. And on the way, Jesus meet Simon, a man from Cyrene, who helped Him make the journey by carrying His cross.

Carrying His Cross

There are two very important lessons here for all who would follow Jesus. First, Jesus made it clear that following Him would be costly. The Christian life brings enormous blessing. The greatest of these are certainly the gifts of intimacy with the Lord, conformity to His image, security in the identity as God's children, and the opportunity to become healing servants. Such blessings are priceless and transformational to all who believe. But Jesus never once hid the fact that the Christian life would be demanding and costly.

Jesus warned people that to follow Him would mean persecution. Family members and friends might reject them, religious powers oppose them, and political systems put them to death. Jesus told His disciples that there were no special privileges for making the journey with Him. And he encouraged people to truly consider the cost before starting out, because turning back was not a proper choice (Luke 9:57-62). When Peter opposed Jesus as He spoke of suffering at the hands of the chief priests, Jesus rebuked him. He told Peter that every person who followed Christ would feel the weight of the cross, and be called to acts of self-denial and sacrifice along the way. If they hoped to avoid this fate and try to save themselves, the consequences could be eternal (Matt. 16:21-28). Jesus was clear that following Him would be costly, and all Christians must take His words seriously when the time comes to choose.

Christians who gather to celebrate the Lord's Supper should seriously think about what the bread and wine represent. Certainly it is a reminder of Christ and His sacrifice, a celebration of the Lord's gift of life. But there is more for believers to consider in the symbols of bread and wine. Within the Eucharistic event is a call to personal sacrifice for the cause of Christ. Wheat must be crushed to become bread that nourishes. Grapes need to be crushed to become wine that refreshes. And Christians must be willing to be broken to serve those who are lost and without Christ.

Mission always involves personal sacrifice. Christians will be called to give time, money, personal dreams, careers, and even children for the Lord's work. Many believers will be wounded along the way, and then use those wounds as a

> *Jesus never once hid the fact that the Christian life would be demanding and costly.*

place of service to others. Some Christians will suffer so that others can be healed and set free. And in certain circumstances some will even be called to give their lives. It was the way of Jesus, and Christians who choose to follow must always keep this reality in mind.

Second, Christians must recognize that not everyone will respond positively to their choice to follow Jesus. He wanted nothing but good for people. He cared about the lost, wanted to set prisoners free, worked to provide for the poor, and healed many people. He had no hidden agenda to gain political or religious power, and was totally uninterested in money and possessions. He loved everyone and treated even the simplest people with great dignity and honor. And in spite of all that, people came against Him. Many did not understand what He was about, others were "fair weather friends," and when things were tough He found Himself alone with God. All hell broke loose against Jesus, not because He was wrong, but because He was doing what was right.

This will happen to Christians as well. Not everyone will understand the journey Christians choose to make. People will assign impure motives, make judgments that are totally inaccurate, and undermine believers best efforts. Spiritual forces will seek to bring oppression and opposition against believers who are trying to give all to Christ. And this will not happen because Christians are doing something wrong. This part of the struggle comes because they are doing what is good and right.

This reality should be made clear to people before they ever consider this journey. Many Christians are not prepared for this part of the Christian life because all they heard when coming to Christ was pie in the sky. The reality of the costly nature of the faith was withheld, and when the time of trial came, they were unnecessary victims who were deeply wounded and discouraged. They said yes to the benefits, but were not made aware that there is a cost. Many who begin to experience the darkness of trial and rejection look to blame themselves. They wonder what they might have done wrong to deserve all this opposition. They need to know that such difficulties come, even at times when they are doing precisely what Jesus commanded. They are being loving, generous, faithful, and true, and yet storms rise against them. It happens, and when it does Christians need to look to Christ who walks closely beside them, because He knows this way very well.

Facing A Crossroads

The Christian journey always goes by way of the cross. Jesus still bears the scars of that path and those who choose to follow must recognize the significance of that. As with Simon of Cyrene, there will always be a cross to bear. There will be sacrifice and self-denial for believers. There was for Jesus and there will be for all who choose to walk with Christ. The type and degree of sacrifice will vary, but Christians must anticipate that there may be a heavy price. People will bring opposition, and some will hate Christians even to the point of death.

Why then choose this fork in the road? Because Jesus is there, waiting to give Himself to all who decide to follow. He is the Treasure for which Christians willingly give all things. He is love and life, and if sacrifice is part of the journey, then so be it. He promises to be with Christians even in the difficulty, for He knows the way well and will give strength for the journey. Some of the sacrifice comes just because Christians have chosen to walk that way. But part of it happens so that others can hear and join the community of Christ on the journey. It is all part of His plan.

Is there another path, a fork in this road? Many would say yes. There are Christians who would have people believe that people can be disciples of Christ without sacrifice. Others even have the notion that being a Christian gives people the right to name and claim more possessions and favor from God. It is a popular notion and many take that path. But they will never find Jesus there, because He went the way of the cross. And Christ clearly said that to follow Him involves the potential for that same level of sacrifice for those closest to Him.

Years ago the great Christian missionary to India, Amy Carmichael, penned a poem about this reality. It serves as a fitting conclusion to this discussion.

No Scar?

Has thou no scar?
No hidden scar on foot, or side, or hand?
I hear thee sung as mighty in the land,
I hear them hail thy bright ascendant star,
Has thou no scar?

Has thou no wound?
Yet I was wounded by the archers, spent,
Leaned Me against a tree to die; and rent
By ravening beasts that encompassed Me, I swooned:
Hast thou no wound?

No wound? no scar?
Yet, as the Master shall the servant be,
And pierced are the feet that follow Me;
But thine are whole: can he have followed far
Who has no wound nor scar?

14 / Crown

A s I was writing this chapter, I received a message from a friend informing me that Gene Evans, a dear saint, left this life earlier that morning and was now in the presence of Christ. Gene Evans' impact upon my own Christian journey is inestimable. His son Evan has been one of my closest friends since my freshman year at Geneva College. I met Gene that year when he and his dear wife Cleo were home from Viet Nam on missionary furlough. He was then, and is now, the most interesting and delightful man I have ever met. I was not following Christ when I met Gene those thirty-one years ago, but from the very first moment he treated my like a son. His enthusiasm for life impressed me, as well as his willingness to spend his days serving as a missionary for Jesus Christ, first in China, and then for twenty-seven years in Viet Nam.

I loved to spend time with Gene. He told the greatest stories. Even when I had heard them several times before, he always told them as if he were recalling those treasured memories for the first time. He laughed harder than anyone at his own jokes, which was more delightful than the jokes themselves. Gene always made me feel special. In fact, I always felt that I was his favorite non-family-member friend. Everyone who knew Gene felt exactly the same way. Gene helped me through a very difficult time several years ago, and I will be forever grateful. I felt loved around him, and am convinced that I was, in fact, experiencing Jesus loving me through him. I can see Gene's smile, feel his big arms wrapped around me, and hear him say as he always did when we parted, "Remember that I love you." Gene, I will never forget!

I will miss Gene Evans, but know that I will see him again. Someday we will meet on the other side, possibly at the eastern gate. And when our eyes meet I expect to hear

---

Jesus is alive and reigns today at the right hand of God Almighty.

---

those familiar words, "Hold the phone, there's Terry." I can almost see it now. What joy that reunion will be! I know this will happen because today, though Gene has gone from this earth, he is actually more alive than I am. Gene is with Jesus. He has finished the course, he has kept the faith, and I am sure he has heard those words, "Well done, my good and faithful servant." Gene chose well along life's path and for him the journey has reached its destination. He has made it home to be with Jesus.

The Reality of the Resurrection

How can a Christian be so sure that there is really life after death and an eternal life with Jesus Christ. The answer is foundational to the Christian faith. Jesus arose from the dead! His body did not degenerate into dust over the centuries that have passed since He walked this earth. He is alive and reigns today at the right hand of God Almighty. When Mary Magdalene went to the tomb that Sunday morning, she was going to anoint Christ's dead body with spices. She saw Him die on the cross and fully anticipated grieving over His corpse that day. But the grave could not hold Jesus, and He arose to live again. When Mary saw Jesus alive she was overjoyed and went running to tell the disciples. They thought she was nuts and wrote it all off as hallucinations.

Later Jesus appeared to the disciples also and even rebuked them for their unbelief. He was alive! (Mark 16:1-20) Jesus went on to walk among them for another forty days, meeting with the disciples behind closed doors (John 22:19-22), on the road to Emmaus (Luke 24:13-35), and by the sea of Tiberias (John 21:1). He showed Thomas his scars (John 20:24-31), and even shared a meal with his followers by the beach (John 21:1-14).

Jesus went on to give His followers final instructions about reaching the nations with the gospel. And then, on the Mount of Olives, Jesus was supernaturally taken into heaven right before their very eyes (Acts 1:1-11). The disciples were transformed by the experience. In the months and years to come their faith in the power of the resurrection did not waver, even in the face of great persecution and, for most of them, torturous deaths. The resurrection was so important that from that day until this, Christians have gathered on the first day of the week to worship a Risen Savior, Jesus Christ the Lord. Believers celebrate Easter every Sunday morning and affectionately refer to it as "The Lord's Day."

The Meaning of the Resurrection

What does all this mean for Christians today? To begin with, the resurrection proved that Jesus was who He said He was. Many people have claimed to be divine over the years. What makes their claims any less valid than those of Jesus

Christ? And if they were quickly dismissed as living under psychological delusions of grandeur, why should Jesus be considered to be sane? There must be an answer, because these are honest questions that hit right at the heart of religious beliefs. To not address these questions simply causes Christians to appear weak minded and somewhat gullible.

But there is an answer and it is the resurrection. Paul wrote in Romans that Jesus was declared, with power, to be the Son of God by His resurrection from the dead. Paul followed that statement with three life-changing words: "Jesus is Lord" (Rom. 1:4). This means that the resurrection of Jesus is proof positive that Jesus was in fact God's Son. He came as a love gift from the Father to give all who believe eternal life. Because of the resurrection Christians should not only trust His words, but follow Him as Lord of their lives. The resurrection proved once and for all that Jesus did die for sin and that the sacrifice He made was pleasing and acceptable before God. And His way of life is the way of life, the only path that leads to everlasting love.

The Power of The Resurrection

The Apostle Paul said that God wants Christians to know that the power that raised Jesus from the dead is at work in all who walk with the Lord (Eph. 1:18, 19). He prayed constantly that Christians would come to see that reality with the eyes of their hearts and be filled with hope. Believers need to stop and contemplate prayerfully what Paul is saying. Christians have a rich inheritance coming to them from the Lord, and some of those gifts are available right here and now. And one of those realized blessings is the incomparable resurrection power that resides within every believers life. This power is, according to Paul, equivalent to the mighty strength God exerted when He raised Jesus from the dead (Eph. 1:20). That concept is very difficult for believers to grasp, yet it is true.

A few years ago I spent some time with a young woman who was raised in a very powerful satanic cult. She recently came to Christ and is on fire for the Lord and being daily changed by his love. In our conversation Becky told me that her family walked in incredible power as they served the evil one. She also said that her sensitivity to spiritual forces had been keenly developed as a member of that cult. And what astounded her was the degree of power she experienced around Christians. "But," she said, "they do not seem to know what they have." That is precisely what Paul was saying. Christians are the temple of the Holy Spirit (I Cor. 7:19). The Spirit of the resurrection dwells in every single believer, which should cause great courage and determination to well up within us. Christians should not be like those who cower back and faint away in battle. Instead, Jesus Christ has given believers resurrection power to move forward and take the high ground in His name.

The Lord's Resurrection Reign

Where is Jesus right now? He is seated at the right hand of the Father. And, according to Paul, He ascended to that position by God's resurrection power. Christians should realize that Christ's position in the heavenlies has direct consequences for their lives. First, it means that Jesus is in charge. Paul wrote that Jesus is above every power in heaven and earth, and that is not only true for now, but forever. God has also placed all things under His feet, and Jesus is head over everything, reigning powerfully for the church (Eph. 1:20-23).

Jesus, the One who loves them as none other and walks daily to draw them into deeper experiences of intimacy, is in charge of everything. Talk about knowing someone! This is the ultimate example of having an inside connection. Christians are close to the Lord of all the universe, who is reigning at the right hand of God! And this mighty Christ has invited believers to ask Him for what they truly need (John 16:23). Jesus provides Christians with a direct link to God the Father, and assures them that He cares about their requests.

Second, with Christ at the right hand of God, Christians have an advocate always standing for them. Scripture says that Jesus is able to completely save anyone who comes to the Father through Him. That same passage teaches believers that Jesus "Always lives to intercede for them" (Heb. 7:24, 25). Jesus, the Living Lord of the Universe, Precious Son of God, Lamb without spot or blemish, Prince of Peace, and Bread of Life, lives to intercede for His followers.

This teaching is almost unfathomable. Christ lives at the right hand of God to serve as a bridge between Christian need and Divine Provision. He does this willingly, joyfully, because He loves His followers and wants to provide the best for them. Any thought that God has abandoned Christians is a lie from the pits of darkness. The very opposite is true. Believers are being watched over and provided for 24/7 by none other than Jesus, the resurrected Christ.

Third, and most amazingly of all, Christians are seated with Christ even now, in heavenly places. Paul wrote that Christians have received incredible gifts from God's grace, not the least of which is being raised up with Christ and seated with Him in glory. Believers generally understand that Jesus dwells within them by the Holy Spirit. But not all Christians know that they are also in Christ as he sits at the right hand of God. This gives believers authority to act in His name and power here on earth. I regularly teach people, when praying, to claim that they are doing so from their position with Christ in the heavenlies.

Both power and authority have been bestowed to Christ's followers through this gracious reality. Believers can speak against the powers of darkness, pronounce blessing, and invite angelic help from above. They can pray for the sick, commission workers, and move forward to advance the cause of the kingdom. While that may to some seem presumptuous, to those who believe it is a privilege of being a follower of Christ. And with that gift comes the awesome responsibility to exercise authority and power according to the spirit and tenderness of Jesus Christ the Lord.

The Promise of the Resurrection

Jesus assured all His followers that He was going ahead to the Kingdom of God to prepare a place for them. He said that Christians should trust Him, because He wants His disciples to be with Him forever (John 14:1-4). This is the promise of the resurrection for every follower of Christ. Jesus said that He was the resurrection and the life, and even if believers die, they will live with Him (John 11:25). This is the sure hope of all who believe. One day, Jesus will come for every person who chose to walk the journey of life with Him. He will meet them either in death or catch them up in the air at His great Second Coming. And at that time, there will be a great celebration that they have reached their eternal home.

There will be a day when all tears will cease, because pure love flows freely to all. Evil will be destroyed and sin will be no more. People will find rest from the long journey, and experience the Presence of Christ, the Eternal Lover. There will be a great city, where the glory of God shines day and night, and people of all tongues, and tribes, and nations will worship together in harmony, singing Glory, and Honor, and Power to the Lamb. Wars will be over, temptation will have ended, and the church, the bride, will be wed to Jesus forever.

The Final Crossroad

The way of least resistance is, at the final hour of life, the road to eternal darkness. It is not pleasant to say, but a reality just the same. Those who go through death's portal without

Christ will stand to be judged on their own merits, not His. Jesus offered to be Lord during life, but for those who refuse, He will not force Himself upon them in death. They will go on alone. There will be no advocate, no interceding voice, no one who will say, "This person belongs to me." There will be only judgment—and silence. Forever. The very thought of this should send Christians out telling everyone about Jesus, and the journey to Life.

But as Christians come to the final shore they will see Jesus more clearly than ever before. This fork in the road leads to the final path, that takes Christians beyond the sacred veil and into the Presence of God. The One who walked with them through this life will take them safely to that other side. His presence, I am sure, will take away the fear of not knowing the way. Many times in life He has walked His followers through to safe ground. He will do so all the more in death. His hand will extend to help us all on the final path, toward home.

My friend Gene Evans is home tonight. I am convinced it is more wonderful than even he could have imagined. Old friends probably greeted him, like the Thompsons, Betty Olsen, Bob Ziemer, and the Griswalds who were all martyred in Viet Nam, and a host of others whose names are precious to bring to mind. For the past two weeks Gene was not conscious of those around him, though family and friends were there to stay close and show their love and devotion. Gene couldn't speak. But several times those nearby saw his lips form a familiar name. It was the name Jesus. The One who was with Him in life, met Gene in death, a beautiful promise of hope for all who still must move ahead on the journey, growing closer to the Lord we love.

Suggested Reading

Bickle, Mike. *Passion for Jesus*. Orlando, FL: Creation House, 1993.

Brown, Stephen. *Approaching God*. Nashville, TN: Moorings, 1996.

Curtis, Brent and John Eldredge. *The Sacred Romance*. Nashville, TN: Thomas Nelson, 1997.

de Caussade, Jean-Pierre. *Sacrament of the Present Moment*. San Francisco, CA: Harper Collins, 1989.

Fenelon, Francois. *The Seeking Heart*. Beaumont, Texas: Seed Sowers, 1992.

Fitz-Gibbon, Andy & Jane. *The Kiss of Intimacy*. Crowborough, England: Monarch, 1995.

Foster, Richard. *Celebration of Discipline*. San Francisco, CA: Harper, 1988.

_____. *Prayer: Finding the Heart's True Home*. San Francisco, CA: HarperCollins, 1992.

Gire, Ken. *Windows of the Soul*. Grand Rapids, MI: Zondervan, 1996.

Guyon, Jeanne. *Experiencing the Depths of Jesus Christ*. Beaumont, Texas: Seed Sowers, 1975.

Lewis, C. S. *The Great Divorce.* New York: MacMillan, 1975.

Manning, Brennan. *The Signature of Jesus.* Sisters, OR: Multnomah,1988.

Miller, Calvin. *Into the Depths of God.* Minneapolis, MN: Bethany House, 2000.

Mulholland, Robert. *Shaped by the Word.* Nashville, TN: Upper Room, 1985.

_____. *Invitation to a Journey.* Downers Grove, ILL: InterVarsity, 1993.

Muto, Susan. *Late Have I Loved Thee.* New York: Crossroads, 1995.

Nouwen, Henri. *Life of the Beloved.* New York: Crossroads, 1992.

_____. *Return of the Prodigal Son.* New York: Image, 1994.

_____. *The Inner Voice of Love.* New York: Doubleday, 1996.

_____.*The Way of the Heart.* San Francisco, CA: Harper SanFrancisco, 1991.

Smith, James Bryan. *Embracing the Love of God.* San Francisco, CA: HarperSanFrancisco, 1995.

St. John of the Cross. *Dark Night of the Soul.* New York: Image, 1990.

Thomas a Kempis. *Of the Imitation of Christ.* PA: Whitaker House, 1981.

Tozer, A. W. *The Pursuit of God.* Camp Hill, PA: Christian Publications, 1982.

_____. *Knowledge of the Holy.* New York: Harper & Brothers, 1961.

Wardle, Terry. *Draw Close to the Fire.* Grand Rapids, MI: Chosen, 1998.

_____. *The Soul's Journey Into God's Embrace.* Ashland, OH: Sandberg Leadership Center, 2000.

Willard, Dallas. *The Spirit of the Disciplines.* New York; Harper & Row, 1988.

_____. *The Divine Conspiracy.* San Francisco, CA: Harper SanFrancisco, 1998.

_____. *Renovation of the Heart.* Colorado Springs, CO: NavPress, 2002.

Also by Terry Wardle

a powerful new tool for pastoral care

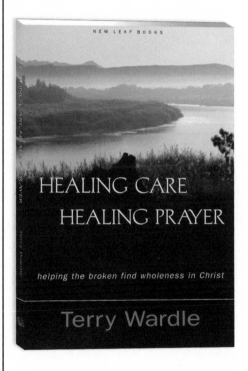

"Caregivers who long to participate in God's ministry of soul transformation will find reliable help here because Terry gives us not just good insight but practices that work."

–Dr. Ken Blue, author of
Authority to Heal

"An excellent book on how to partner with Jesus, working in his power and authority, to go beyond the mere understanding of our problems to healing, to freedom."

–Dr. Charles H. Kraft, Fuller Theological Seminary

255 pages, softcover   *$15.99*

1-877-634-6004 toll free

If you or someone you know is interested in attending a seminar with Dr. Terry Wardle, contact him at:

Healing Care Ministries
P.O. Box 933
Ashland, Ohio 44805
twardle@ashland.edu